At Home
on the Road

To
Toby and Inge, who always encourage me
Rachel, who made her own journeys
and
Bill, who is with me every step of the way.

At Home
on the Road
Jill Malcolm

NEW
HOLLAND

First published in 2002 by New Holland Publishers (NZ) Ltd
Auckland • Sydney • London • Cape Town

218 Lake Road, Northcote, Auckland, New Zealand
14 Aquatic Drive, Frenchs Forest, NSW 2086, Australia
86–88 Edgware Road, London W2 2EA, United Kingdom
80 McKenzie Street, Cape Town 8001, South Africa

www.newhollandpublishers.co.nz

ISBN: 1 877246 63 8

Publishing manager: Matt Turner
Editor: Alison Dench
Cover design: Sue Attwood
Cover illustration: Paul Fletcher
Design and typesetting: Alison Dench

10 9 8 7 6 5 4 3 2

Printed by McPherson's Printing Group, Australia

Contents

Acknowledgements

A special thanks for my beloved children, Inge and Toby, who have always said in response to their mother's wild ideas, 'You must go and do it at once.' I thank my much-loved daughter, Rachel, who lives on in spirit and who said to me before she left, 'Life is a great thing as you know. Be happy.' A loving thank-you to Bill, who is my rock and who makes our journeys and exploration together possible.

I thank my aunt, the late Dorothea Joblin, who with her own writings inspired me. In the chapter 'The Point of Going' I have quoted a short passage from one of her books, *Harvey Come Quick*.

I'd also like to acknowledge with thanks: Liz Parker of *Next* magazine, who commissioned the first article about our journey; Bernice Beachman, who first suggested I write a book; Renée Lang of New Holland, who has supported the project with such enthusiasm; the production and marketing team at New Holland for their hard work; and Alison Dench who energetically undertook the tasks of editing and typesetting.

I also thank the people around New Zealand who wittingly or unwittingly allowed me glimpses of their lives and who coloured and enriched our travels with their humour, hospitality, ingenuity and appreciation of their own country.

Why Not?

The road, shining like a freshly ironed ribbon, drew us on. Bill tinkered with the wing mirror of the truck to check on the progress of the caravan. He frowned slightly as it jibbed around one of the sharper corners. 'We'll have to stop soon and balance the load a bit,' he said. 'We need more weight up the front.'

I was studying the hills – how the clouds leaked down like tears from the pyramid peaks into the great rocky crevices and the mustard-coloured tussock covering the flanks looked like pilled blankets. Behind the hills the monumental presence of the mountains made our own seem tiny and inconsequential. Beside the road a river that had been skipping merrily over its stony bed suddenly flopped into a deep pool where, below the dark surface of the water, the eddies and undercurrents swirled unseen like malicious gossip.

I yawned and tried to locate the moment that had led us to these giant hills, on the road to everywhere and nowhere. Perhaps a seed was sown in a throw-away line while we were dropping off to sleep in front of the television, or when we were picking up the contents of the rubbish bin that someone else's dog had distributed over the lawn, or maybe during the hellish drive to work in Auckland's traffic on a Monday morning.

Somehow the idea of embarking on a life on the road evolved.

At first we rolled the thought around lightheartedly. Then, over the next few months, there were gradual and subtle changes. We started saying 'when we' instead of 'if we were to' and 'we must' instead of 'maybe we could'.

We mentioned it to others in passing – putting a finger up to test the wind. 'We've decided to become nomadic,' I told friends with a flippancy I didn't always feel. 'We're going to throw a few belongings in a caravan and depart. It's called buggering off.' Their responses were more like a gusty nor'wester than an onshore breeze. 'What on earth do you want to do that for?' or 'A bit off the wall if you ask me,' or 'You'll never last the distance.' Disapproval was powerful fuel for a rebellious nature, and such lack of enthusiasm, far from putting us off, set the thing in concrete. Almost without our noticing, dreams became plans.

A friend asked me to meet her for lunch and over cups of foamy coffee in a Ponsonby café her mood suddenly changed from jocular to earnest. 'Everything's here – your friends, your home, your job opportunities. We'll all miss you, you know, and you've been through the wringer lately. Do you really want to rock the boat again?'

'I'm not rocking the boat,' I said with a firmness that hid my own reservations. 'I'm jumping right out of it.'

'But tell me *why* are you doing this caravan thing,' she said.

Until that moment I hadn't even thought of a reason. If I had to come up with one I might have referred to nomadic urges that had lingered since I'd wandered around Africa with Iain, my first husband. We were in our late twenties then. He was a doctor and I was a physiotherapist, and we had worked and travelled all over that stupendous continent for four years. Whenever we could jingle a few coins together we would take off into the wilds in our navy-coloured Volkswagen, with a pup tent for accommodation, so that we could photograph birds. We had no reason then and almost no money. But it was one of the richest times of my life.

Perhaps to go without reason was precisely the point. When I looked back on the too-many decades that I'd already lived, I could see that most of the things that had happened in my life had been random. I'd been to plenty of work seminars about goal-setting, but my arrival at some particular point was usually accompanied by a feeling of astonishment at being there rather than the satisfaction of having achieved a particular goal. And so the intention Bill and I had – to roam, to allow circumstances and whim to lead us by the nose, to learn about living without meaning or purpose and see how it felt – was well within my zone of comfort.

The project took on a momentum of its own. Brick walls tumbled as if fate had taken over. Bill, who had been unsettled as a commercial real-estate agent, left work without much apparent regret. Some of my good friends were distancing or moving on and my three children, who had been the light of my life, had already left home. Two of them, Inge and Toby, were more or less self-sufficient. I found an excellent home for Trixie, the family pony, in Albany with a five-year-old who adored her and fed her carrots on the hour. My daughter's old thoroughbred gelding became ill and had to be helped to greener pastures. Oscar the cat had become too old and feeble to live happily.

Inwardly, however, I was more than a little shaky. I had moments of quiet panic at the thought of ever leaving the cosy security of home. What if we couldn't find work or we hated it and couldn't come back or we couldn't stand the sight of each other after a month of close confinement? And we hadn't great reserves in the bank should things go wrong. On the other hand it was now or never, and that thought made me braver. Without saying much about it, Bill and I both knew that this could be our last chance. As we got older there was always the thought that sickness or some other sort of decrepitude could sneak up at any moment. We kept hearing of people who were 'only our age' being handicapped by some sort of crippling age-related thing. Some had already departed for that other great unknown.

Eventually, in the absence of a reason to go there was not much reason to stay. But there was a stronger catalyst that I took a while to admit to – the deep-down, unarticulated feeling that geographical removal might somehow rid me of some of the pain.

Rachel died. There, I've written it, but suddenly the computer screen has developed wavering watermarks. I can't see those two words because my vision is blurred with tears. Years later anything that brings me close to the reality still sets me off – crying in a way that only a mother who has outlived a child can cry. She was my eldest daughter and she was on Santorini Island in Greece, trying to make sense of her world, twenty-three years of age, pretty, blonde with an unpredictable temper and a well-developed sense of humour, and she died of internal bleeding from a cause that was never identified. Grief still sometimes invades me, wrapping around my mind and rummaging in my chest until every bit of courage or resolution or acceptance dissolves and I am left teetering on the edge of a yawning gap that nothing will ever be able to fill.

Work helped me face the world again. Then Bill sidled into my life about six months later and, despite all the havoc and heartache entangling me, seemed to want to stay around. He made me laugh and organised me and made me feel that I could enjoy things again. We'd been living together for a year or more when the idea of this odyssey germinated and grew.

The die was irrevocably cast when I was on an assignment in San Francisco. Bill rang me to say he had found the perfect caravan. 'It's an Anglo Astral,' he said. 'Five-point-five metres long, twenty years old and in need of a bit of care, but only ten thousand bucks.'

It wasn't a thing of great beauty. Its shape was a bit like an over-risen loaf of bread, and running down either flank was a broad stripe the colour of weak tea. Some of its edges had had a battering – but then so had mine. It was quite roomy inside, with a small table that could be extended. Down one wall was a squabbed bench seat and on the opposite side of the table was a smaller one. There was a skinny wardrobe, and lying across the caravan against the back window was a double bed. The bench was L-shaped and covered in a mottled, mustard-coloured formica. Set into this was a sink that was so small you could hardly dunk a doughnut in it. Any other space was taken up with cupboards and drawers. The carpet was a ghastly chocolate brown and the cushions and decorative touches a kind of nipple pink. Set into a small divide between the bench and the wardrobe and in a panel in the door was the rippled, beer-bottle glass that was fashionable in the sixties.

'That will have to go,' I announced firmly, 'and so will that carpet and the cushions. I'm not living with those.' It took about a month to replace the cushions, and another three to get around to the carpet. We never replaced the glass.

Three weeks later we bought a Nissan Safari, a roaring black Darth Vader of a vehicle with plenty of grunt for pulling. Perched high off the ground surrounded by its solid frame, I discovered I had suddenly gained a lot of respect from the lesser vehicles on the road – size really did matter. We had decided that we would also take Bill's old Mercedes with us. Neither of us was prepared to give up vehicular independence and if we were both working we'd need two cars.

Bill took me down to the local supermarket car park late at night to practise backing the caravan. I had to weave it around buckets placed on the ground, which felt a bit like pushing an elephant backwards through a keyhole. After many attempts and a few squashed buckets, Bill's instructions became gradually louder and muffled behind clenched teeth. 'Left hand down. Left hand. Left hand, God in heaven. Left. Put your right hand behind your back, woman. That's it. Now right…not that much…left, left.' At that point any sense of direction in reverse that I might have gained deserted me completely. At the end of a week of practice I still wasn't sure which way the damned thing was going to go. It couldn't seem to make up its mind.

Next I left work. Actually it left me. I'd been the editor of the Air New Zealand inflight magazine, *Pacific Wave*, for eleven years and was made redundant with the rest of the staff when Australian Consolidated Press (NZ) lost the publishing contract to an Australian publishing company. I was not seriously dismayed: eleven years was a good run. I'd had a frantic, exhilarating and productive time travelling, writing, organising, managing and feeling that I might be making a difference.

It had been a good way to earn a living to be sure, but insidious changes had taken place. I found I was often spending time with people whose attitude to life was far removed from my own. And somewhere along the way it had all started to feel a bit meaningless, as if reality – mine at least – was elsewhere. I'd already asked myself if this was what I wanted to be doing. The answer was that I didn't want to spend the next ten years in the same way that I had spent the last. Then the airline's decision took away the need for me to make my own.

My biggest regret was leaving my colleagues. They had for so long been my daytime family that I missed them dreadfully. It was a bit like being thrown out of home and, like an adolescent, one half of me felt excited and bold and the other half insecure and abandoned.

Bill and I spent the next three months primping the house and garden to a level it had never seen before. We off-loaded about half our possessions. A couple of garage sales emphasised that they weren't worth much anyway. I hated throwing things out so I learnt the trick of leaving useable things at the front gate. By morning they were nearly always gone. One foggy evening I watched through my lounge window the bulky figure of a man dipping rhythmically into the pile, rolling each item over like a foraging turnstone. A cellphone was jammed against his ear. He shuffled off and dissolved into the darkness and a few minutes later a van pulled up. Out jumped a leaner figure – one of those small rigid men who when they bend forward look as if they are going to tip over. He swooped on my pile, hurled it into the back of the van and was gone. It was like watching a pantomime behind a gauze curtain. They were back again the next night. I hoped they were putting our things to good use.

The upheaval of all this organisation was enormous. It seemed odd that I had spent the first half of my life trying to upsize my lifestyle and increase my worldly goods and here I was squashing them down to minimal proportions. We were ruthless about the amount we took with us because in a caravan we had to consider not only volume but also weight. I wondered how we would survive with so little – and found out later that we had more than we needed.

We arranged tenants who turned out to be excellent caretakers. Elizabeth and Neil Myburgh, their two daughters Simoné and Danielle, and Elizabeth's mother Rita had recently arrived from South Africa where, they said, the violence had become unbearable. Rita's husband and son had been randomly shot dead at their Pretoria service station. Elizabeth had been mugged a week before she left for New Zealand. We agreed that they would move into the house the day after we left.

Ebony was the last to go. She was our much loved sixteen-year-old kelpie dog, and even though she wasn't very well, I just couldn't face the thought of putting her down. Two days before deadline Owen, who was doing some last-minute gardening for us, asked what I was going to do with her. I dissolved into tears.

'You're not?' he said in a horrified tone.

'I haven't got an option.'

'I'll take her. Our old dog has just died and my boys really miss him. I'd be happy to have Ebony and so will they. I'll look after her, I promise.'

I was so grateful I had to stop myself from wringing his hand and tugging my forelock.

Two days later Ebony went off with the gardener. She jumped into the front seat of his truck and took happy possession. I stared through the window into her eyes, trying to figure out how she was feeling – if I could detect any doggy intuition that let her know we were parting. Her eyes gave me nothing. She yawned luxuriously and curled her tongue. The next time I saw her was two days before she died.

Bill and I cut off the phone, the electricity, the paper delivery and the security alarm in preparation to cast off. At ten-thirty on the morning of the 13th of January I walked to the car with just one glance at the oddly neat house standing silent and barren in the sunlight. There was no one to wave goodbye. It was as if I'd never lived there.

Friends and Enemies

We spent our first days in an inner-city caravan park adjusting to the change and finishing odd bits of business that we hadn't got around to. It was immediately apparent that our social status had altered when Bill bargained with the manager for the best ten-day deal. 'That's the trouble with the likes of you,' the woman muttered, throwing me a withering glance, 'always on the scrounge.' I opened my mouth to throw her an indignant one-liner and found there was nothing to say. We got a couple of dollars off the price.

It was our first lesson in how life on the road could have its image problems. Containing the whiff of the impoverished, the suspect and the ostracised, the very words 'gypsy' and 'nomad' had long been put-downs. This ancient response revealed the ignorance of those who uttered it – the nomads we were to meet around New Zealand were nearly all spirited, interesting and admirable, even if they were among the country's lowest earners.

The anti attitude may have come from a yearning for the money and success that we were told in myriad ways was the path to happiness. If we wanted to fit in we must be seen to upscale our wealth and stability, or at least let it be known that we had transcendent aspirations. Nomads were motivated not by success but by survival. It seemed a perfectly valid way of living a life, at least as valid as a life spent sipping latte with a cellphone jammed to your ear, driving the company BMW like a kamikaze pilot or dressing in designer gear in order to proclaim to anyone watching that you are, indeed, on the way up.

Our new home was tightly jammed up against a gypsy truck with coloured leadlight windows and perished tyres, in which lived a gloriously handsome, dark-skinned Adonis with a pony tail and melting black eyes. Every morning he stripped to the waist and practised jujitsu on the grass. I couldn't take my eyes off him.

Cheek by jowl on the other side of us, a campervan housed Carol and Merl from England. At precisely six o'clock each evening they brought out a round plastic table from the van, placed it on their tiny outdoor patch, covered it with a blue tablecloth, and set it with a vase of artificial roses, a bottle of wine, a dish of peanuts and two matching wine glasses. Then they sat opposite each other solemnly imbibing until the bottle was empty, a ritual conducted in complete silence. They both looked as contented as if those shabby surroundings were in fact the Fiji Sheraton and they were sipping fruity cocktails under the shade of palm trees by the lapping tide.

Some of my friends came for coffee and parked their new, expensive-looking vehicles close to the caravan. The manager was very pleasant after that and smilingly wished us a safe journey when we paid the bill a few days later. We pulled out of the caravan park and drove onto the motorway south and the city began to fall behind us. Driving Bill's car behind the caravan, I could observe, with some anxiety, the ponderous progress down the motorway of our entire household. I felt vaguely detached, as if the reality was still an imagining.

Daylight was already receding when we rumbled into the Lake Taupo Top 10 Holiday Park, which was in caravan park terms a five-star resort. We found a plot isolated from the common herd in an area called Lusty Flats. And ten minutes later a green-striped caravan pulled by a small pick-up settled in almost alongside us.

'Nosy parkers,' Bill grumbled.

At this early stage of our roaming life we had not yet perfected the ritual of setting up the caravan. First the jacks on the four corners had to be wound down to make contact with the earth and keep the caravan stable. Levelling was important if you didn't want to have everything inside the caravan sliding in one direction. We did this with a spirit level, unlike the experts who could do it by eye. The water hose had to be attached, to the caravan inlet at one end and to the tap at the other. Too bad if you lost the tap attachment or had the wrong size. The electricity was connected and the aerial for the television hoisted above the roof and the cable threaded through a small window above the bed. All the items that had been floored for the journey and all the cushions and towels that I had squeezed into the cupboards to stop the contents moving had to be removed. By the time we'd done all this dusk was upon us.

At the time our neighbours were putting up their awning we were tackling the same task. Erecting a fully enclosed awning, the same size as the caravan, so that all the windows and doors were in the right place was no task for novices. It attached by means of a rope that had to be threaded through a groove in the side of the caravan. Then there were ten inner poles (in bits), fourteen ropes and twenty-six pegs with characteristics varying according to function to be sorted out. It was the sort of exercise that should be given to couples thinking they might want to get married – a truer test of character than getting your partner drunk, which had always been my father's advice for sorting out the men from the boys.

Our neighbours, Tom and Susie, were in trouble. Tom, with a balding head and bristling moustache, was one those little red-faced men who take enormous strides to try to make up for their lack of height.

'Evening,' Bill said to Tom, who'd spread his awning on the grass and was looking at it in a puzzled sort of way.

'Yerp,' Tom replied. We found out later that opening a conversation with Tom was like trying to remove the cork from a wine bottle with your teeth.

As the exercise progressed, Tom became more and more Hitlerian, running his awning-erection operation like a tense military exercise. Susie started twittering, trying to be helpful and getting rebuffed. And the more he bawled the more she twittered.

I was having problems of my own. Dark had descended, and we worked by the light of a full moon. Bill started barking orders: 'Put that down. Not that one, that one. Now pull, hold it. Pull…harder, harder than that. Where's that hammer? Have you moved those pegs? Leave things where they are.' My experience of sailing with them had taught me that when men get into this I-am-in-control-here-you-useless-clod mood, it was best to lie doggo. Do as you're told, say nothing. Of course, I would have liked to pick up a peg and whack him over the ear – but then how would I put up the awning?

Out of the corner of my eye I saw Susie, with the enormous deliberation of contained aggression, place upon the ground the pole she had been holding for Tom, and with a scalding look in his direction, walk slowly from the scene.

What a good idea.

I joined her and this stranger and I exchanged smiles and then, without saying a word, got the giggles. We laughed all the way past the swimming pool and the children's playground and we spluttered our way down the hill to examine the barbecue area and the kitchen, and by the time we got back we were friends.

The awnings were up – both of them. Our fine orange-and-brown striped one was a perfect oblong, erected with hardly a wrinkle. Tom's, I'm sorry to say, was forlornly lopsided. The roof sagged at one end and the whole thing was skew-whiff, as if a mini-hurricane had passed through. Tom was sitting outside in a director's chair drinking beer from a can. He looked pleased with himself. I admired Bill's work and went inside to make dinner, feeling slightly superior.

Next day I set out half an hour after Bill had left with the caravan. Tooling at 110 kilometres per hour across the wide, flat Rangitaiki Plains under a high, bright sky with the road stretching out like a grey belt in front of me, my spirits soared well above the roof of the car. I felt the way I had expected to feel leaving Auckland – unfettered, elated, free. A blues singer crooned on the radio and a warm wind blasted in the window and fingered my hair. I began to sing.

Then up behind me came a dark blue BMW, nudging at me like a cat with a mouse, pulling in too close, swerving out on the road and then falling back and buzzing my tail. When it finally passed the driver scowled at me as if I had impeded her more important progress. I was suddenly furious, my euphoria in tatters. It was not easy for me to get a high and the wretched woman had crushed it.

When I pulled off the road a quarter of an hour later and parked among the birch trees by the Waipunga River, the scowler was there with her car door ajar, munching some morsel. She was in her mid-forties, her hair dark and sleek. The collar of her pink check shirt was turned up around her ears and around her shoulders was slung a navy jersey. She had the look of an organic-soap seller – wholesome and as polished as the gleaming paint of her Beamer. My fury hadn't abated. I leapt out of the car towards her and out of my mouth sprang a question that startled even me.

'Who the hell do you think you are?' I bawled.

No reply required! I spun around and wobbled too fast over the stones to the edge of the stream. I had always been the sort of person who said sorry if someone trod on my toe and so, as I watched thin ribbons of water chattering over the rocks, I wondered if this outburst was the beginning of another sort of liberation.

The woman was still there when I returned to my car. She looked pleasant enough. She saw me coming and shut the door. I smiled, baring my teeth. 'Glorious day,' I said, climbed into the Merc and drove off. I felt marvellously empowered. I'd made one friend and one enemy in the last twenty-four hours and it felt fine.

In my own country not all places were new frontiers. I had travelled this route from Taupo to Hastings since I was ten years old, when we went to Taupo for summer holidays. I remember winding over the gravel road in my father's Zephyr Six Mark II, and having to get out to walk on several of the corners which were too sharp and steep for it to manoeuvre with a full load.

A jumble of recollections, some as blurry as old photographs, rose to the surface. I was in my early twenties when I drove over the Rangitaiki Plains in a heavy fog in my mother's lettuce-green Morris Minor to meet my boyfriend in Taupo. For some reason it was about four o'clock in the morning and a ghostly mist had reduced my world to a few metres in front of the headlights. About half way across the plains something exploded in the innards of the engine and I swerved to the side of the road and stopped.

The fog curled like smoke through the scrub and it was so quiet I could hear my own breathing. It was July and somewhere close to here the notorious prison escaper George Wilder was reported to be on the roam. He was something of a folk hero, breaking in to uninhabited baches for food and shelter, and leaving polite notes of thanks. I half hoped he would and half hoped he wouldn't materialise from the fog. An hour later I was picked up by two men on their way to go fishing in the lake. Four days later George Wilder was also picked up – by the police, who had seen a light in the window of a small hut off the Napier–Taupo road. He'd been on the run for 169 days.

Some way further on I passed the summit, where my family would routinely stop on the five-hour journey to Taupo. We'd pull over onto the bracken at the side of the road and eat cold sausages and tomato sauce wrapped in white bread. I'd usually waste mine by throwing up on the winding second half of the trip but to this day I consider cold sausages and tomato sauce a treat. My father would gather twigs for the thermette, which we used in preference to a thermos so that the tea would be fresh. Now, however, there was a café at the summit and our picnic spot was gone.

Near Te Haroto there was a half-hidden house just off the road where, until a couple of years earlier, Alan McVicar and Wayne Cheer lived. For many years they ran one of the most philanthropic tow truck and mechanical services in the country. They towed my friend Derek's car there once when he and I were travelling together back from Hastings.

Derek's old Toyota had been coughing badly coming over the hills and hissing steam. It broke down completely 5 kilometres down the road from McVicar's. It appeared that Derek, more interested in writing poetry than delving into engines, had not investigated the radiator for several years and it had a very bad dose of rust. His answer to the current dilemma was to kick the sides of the car and beat its bonnet with his fists. It would have been a performance worthy of John Cleese, except that Derek was short and tubby and after a minute or two completely out of breath. I hitched a ride up the road and brought Alan back with his tow truck. Alan and Wayne not only worked cheerfully on the problem for two hours, but plied us with tea and chocolate cake while we waited.

One side of Alan and Wayne's yard, in the preferred decor of most mechanics, was coated with the patina of grime and oil and filled with old cars and rusting car parts; the other was a delicately landscaped garden full of fruit trees. They charged us $40, which was absurdly cheap. Derek gave them $80 and I determined to call in on my way past sometime and take them a cake or some offering of thanks.

I never did go back, and now I found the blue tow truck with 'Alan McVicar, Heavy Salvage Contractor – Wayne Cheer, Towing Services' written on the door abandoned under a large fir tree at the front gate. The house was silent, the windows blank and everywhere there were signs of neglect and decay.

This sort of historical musing filled me with a muted pleasure. 'Have I told you about the time…' I frequently said to Bill. Now that we had been together for five years I invariably had, but sometimes he indulged me. 'About twenty times actually, but why don't you tell me again.'

A Breath of Country Air

In Hawke's Bay we stopped at my sister and brother-in-law's farm among the rolling landscape of Greenhill about 15 kilometres out of Hastings. It was a shake-down time when we could take things quietly, settle into the idea of our new lifestyle and recover from the ordeal of organising it. One of the many good things about caravan life is that you can stay with friends and relatives without the intensity of staying in-house. Wendy and Don didn't have to alter the rhythm of their lives to have us as guests; we spent time together only when we chose to. Sometimes we had dinner with them and sometimes they had dinner with us. I enjoyed the balance between company and self-sufficiency.

Spending time in the Hawke's Bay country brought a rising sense of optimism, which probably had a lot to do with the pleasant time I'd had growing up there. In my early life I had been surrounded by ponies and two-tooth sheep, home-killed mutton and working dogs. I remembered winters of gumboots, mud, oilskins and orphaned baby lambs bunting the rubber teats on the end of the lemonade bottles that we converted into feeding bottles.

Wendy and Don Gordon's farm had none of this. Don had turned more and more to thoroughbred horse breeding on the 24 hectares they hadn't sold off. There were six mares in the front paddock and only a handful of sheep and cattle fattening on the long grass.

We parked the caravan in the dappled shade of a large rhus tree next to an old storage shed. The first night Bill and I decided to eat early and alone, and then drop into bed. We were both feeling drained from making our getaway. As we tucked into fatty pork chops and lettuce salad, thinking how superb the quiet of the countryside was, we heard a sound like little fingers tapping at the windows. Closer inspection revealed dozens of bees bashing themselves against the glass in swooping dives. When we opened the door about twenty of them suddenly found themselves inside and they buzzed maniacally at the windows trying to find their way back out again. They were coming from a hive under the eaves of the shed.

'They've been there for twenty-five years,' Don said later. 'We've smoked them out several times but they always come back.'

For our own selfish reasons we tried to live in peace with the bees. I carefully removed infiltrators with a tea-towel and didn't kill one. They reciprocated by keeping their stings to themselves.

I slipped into country life by taking long walks. At eight in the morning the sun was already sharp, the sky piercing blue. 'It'll be a stinker,' said Neville, who was out watering the agapanthus along his drive. He and his wife Delcie, who had moved to the country for a peaceful lifestyle, lived at the bottom of the hill in a corrugated-iron woolshed they had converted into one of the most livable homes, satisfying in form and proportion, I had encountered. The couple bred donkeys.

Although surrounded by hills, the road that passed Greenhill was flat. I was struck by the stillness and the quiet. It was like a vacuum after the city. A harrier flapped languidly around the grassy slopes looking for breakfast and a herd of cows trotted after me along the fence-line, kicking up puffs of dust that hung in the windless air. When I stopped, they stopped and looked at me, some beseechingly, others with expressions of dopey indignation.

As the morning progressed a few country sounds broke through. A chattering flock of finches hurtled past, magpies echoed their resonant gurgling melodies. Out of sight a farmer was shouting and whistling instructions to his dogs and a small plane buzzed the hills. And then, in the distance, came the faint chewing noise of an approaching car. In that isolated setting it seemed ominous and as it came closer I worked at keeping my imagination under control. Things were not always benign on country roads. I moved well off the tarmac, my spine prickling. It swished past – a pale green Toyota, completely innocent. The driver lifted his finger off the wheel to acknowledge me.

The Gordons' sprawling farmhouse was half way up a hill at the top of which was one of Hawke's Bay's lavishly grand old homesteads. The house had intrigued me from the time I was a flag-waving girl guide. I had not forgotten how the royal standard had fluttered from the tower of the Greenhill homestead when the Queen Mother, visiting New Zealand in 1950, had requested a stay in a home typical of pioneering days. Nor had I forgotten that the city fathers of the day had had the grass mown on either side of the road all the way from Hastings along the route that Her Majesty would take. To my young mind this had been an awe-inspiring gesture.

I was no royalist but the adoration I felt for anything queenly as a young girl nevertheless imbued a sort of mystique on the place where such a personage had stayed. And that had never entirely left me. But the imposing edifice, with its steeple, extensive views and sweeping lawns, was hardly the archetypal dwelling of our forebears, most of whom slogged it out in one-roomed hovels.

The current owner was Cath Wiggins. I rang her and she invited me to call in. In her modernised kitchen she poured two cups of coffee and pushed a tin of home-made Anzac biscuits towards me across the bench. I worked on conjuring up the Arcadian lifestyle that would have existed there early in the twentieth century, when servants were a mark of status.

'Imagine it,' I said to Cath. 'There was probably croquet on the lawn, horse riding and hunting across the estate, billiards in the hall, afternoon tea on the verandahs – sipped delicately, of course, and accompanied by scones, butterfly cakes and cucumber sandwiches presented on three-tiered cake stands...oh, and elaborate dinner parties at the long dining table.'

Cath laughed. 'There's nothing too elegant about living here now.'

Her children were the sixth generation to live there, descendants of the first owners, Archibald and Elizabeth McClean. Time had chipped away at the house, and here and there it was sadly lacking in paint and restoring it would take a bit of coaxing. But it was still solidly there, dignified and stately and a tribute to the consummate care of its builders.

'Actually its upkeep is more than we can handle,' Cath said. 'It's on the market if you're interested.'

There were joyful celebrations going on in Hawke's Bay that weekend, an orgy of wine, art, food and music. My recollections of the Heretaunga Plains were of apple-picking and drafting fat lambs with my father at daybreak, the thick savoury smell of tomato sauce emanating from J Wattie Canneries, of learning how to harvest asparagus by slicing each spear an inch above the ground, and of picking peas into a kerosene tin which, filled to the top, earned me two shillings.

Now the only talk was of grapes and olives, lavender and organics. I drove around some of the wineries, of which there were then around forty, and briefly joined the sybaritic crowds who were in the grip of an overwhelming sense of well-being engendered by the grape, the music and the sun. I marvelled at some of the food combinations – fine ale mustard sauce, minted apple chutney, kiwifruit, orange and lavender jam, lemon and brandy marmalade, quince cheese, sherry wine vinegar, duck confit in aspic (which looked like a lab specimen). In my day it was roast mutton and vegetables on Sunday and chops or mince for the rest of the week.

At one vineyard a young man took it upon himself to give me an impromptu lecture on how to taste wine. The fellow's face seemed to gather into his nose, which was so large that it could not fit inside a normal wine glass but rested on the rim opposite his mouth. When he wanted to drink, therefore, he had to either tip his head back or suck the wine into his mouth by inhaling sharply, which became more difficult the lower the wine in the glass. I was so riveted by his nasal nuisance that I had to force myself to listen to the information he was giving me.

He knew what he was talking about. 'Here, take this,' he said, handing me a half glass of Merlot Cabernet. 'First look at it from above for clarity and depth of colour. Now tip the glass and look at the wine against this white background here. There, do you see its main hue? Swirl it to see its viscosity. Hold the glass at eye level. That indicates the wine's weight. Sniff into the glass, keeping the wine still, and then swirl it and keep smelling until it settles. Vary the relationship of your nose to the glass. Agitate the wine violently to get the heavier, more intense smell.'

I spilled mine. He gave me a pained glance and continued. 'Keep smelling as the wine settles. Now take a sip and distribute the wine all around your palate so that you analyse the initial attack. Swallow a little, aerate it by sucking, swallow a little more and spit out the rest.'

I swallowed the lot.

'Now, breathe through your nose, smack your lips for the final savour and think about the length of taste. Now what did you think of that?'

'Mmmm, very nice,' I said.

I decided that if that was what it took to appreciate wine I could end up on the wagon.

Hawke's Bay was as hot as I could remember it. Melted tar crackled as I drove and when I stepped out of the car the sun hit me like a blow to the head. The desiccated hills, tree-naked, were furry with camel-coloured grass and quivering ripples of light blurred the edges of the distant ranges.

The smell of dust and sun-baked hay reminded me of the time when I was nine and first experienced caravan life. We didn't go to Taupo that year but took a small caravan to the beach at Clifton near Hastings and parked it with others on the spiky grass, in the shadow of the bluff that gave the place its name. On the first night, as my family sat at the formica table to eat, our tiny abode suddenly began to tilt and didn't stop until its belly was rammed against the ground and all four of us were entangled against the back window garnished with mince, mashed potato and peas. I could still see the milk jug hurtling towards me off the bench and bits of shredded lettuce flying through the air. I think I copped the milk and my sister wore most of the caramel pudding.

A crowd soon gathered to exclaim over this happening and several of the men lifted us back on the level by winding down the jacks that should have been lowered in the first place. My mother, brushing gravy from her apron, grabbed the biscuit tin and started handing home-made shortcake around the crowd. Why she did this I didn't understand, but I panicked at the thought that there would be none left for me. The only other things I remembered of the holiday were Johnny Hampton peeing on the feet of Elsie Taylor because she wouldn't give him a bite of her toffee bar and Roger Bosher losing my sister's fishing line in the surf.

After that holiday I did not climb into a caravan for another forty-five years.

An Eager Hooker

After a week in Hawke's Bay the weather changed. A white, neatly demarcated arc of cloud appeared. When he was alive my father had always pointed this out to me. 'Wind's on its way,' he'd say. 'There's the Hawke's Bay arch.'

By two in the afternoon, hot air was roaring through the trees and rocking the caravan ever so slightly, despite its carefully adjusted jacks. Everything altered. Yesterday the countryside had been motionless, stunned into silence by the heat. Now it moved with breathy energy. Willow branches swayed gracefully while the branches of taller trees creaked apart and then slapped together.

I felt energised. I walked along the avenue leading to the road, picking my way among the windy detritus: acorns and pinecones dropped like confetti, branches, strips of bark, one dead baby bird, its primary feathers just beginning to form, and a delicate finch's nest lined with wool and possum fur and walled with twirls of baby fern.

It was still blowing the next day when we left for Napier. The date was the 3rd of February, the sixty-ninth anniversary of the earthquake that in 1931 had broken the city up like so many crushed biscuits. From the crumbs rose the plethora of art deco buildings that today were the reason people found the character of the city so easy to locate. You could put your finger on Napier.

The earthquake, then, was the end and also the beginning. When people in the city referred to periods of time it was either before the earthquake or after the earthquake, in the same way that people said pre-war or post-war. And then there was the 'time of the earthquake'.

On the anniversary of that momentous day, I decided to pay my own form of homage to the event. When we'd settled in to a camping ground for the night I took myself off to the Hawke's Bay Museum, where there was a comprehensive display of the earthquake and its immediate aftermath, including video accounts from survivors. But another item had a stronger resonance for me. I'd been to the museum a few times before, but I couldn't remember seeing that four-by-two piece of timber. Crudely written on it in red paint were a location notice and the names of fourteen people. After the quake people had been too scared to go back to their houses because of the sometimes violent aftershocks and so for several weeks they camped out in open spaces.

CAMP Bluff Hill
Cox's lawn
Feb 1931
Mr Somerset Smith
Enquire Depot
Mrs Somerset Smith
Miss   "   "

– and so on.

There was a faint chance that some people from the Cox's lawn camp could still be alive and, if so, I wanted to talk to them. I started a search by asking the attendant behind the desk at the museum. She put me on to someone else who put me onto someone else and eventually I spoke to a woman who said yes, she knew of a man who could well be one of the family. It took bit of doing, but I tracked down Mr Owen Somerset Smith and his phone number and gave him a call.

'Yes, well, I am what they call a survivor,' he said, 'but I was only thirteen at the time and I don't think my story's very dramatic.'

I wanted to hear it anyway and invited myself to meet him at his house on Bluff Hill. A neatly dressed man of eighty-one opened the door. He had the bearing of a person used to holding authority and who had seen much more in his life than the subject that had brought me there.

'Hello, welcome,' he said. 'Please come in.'

He led the way to his front drawing room, which overlooked the wide sweep of Napier and the part of Hawke Bay that stretched as far as Cape Kidnappers. In the city below us the rows of Norfolk pines along the foreshore and the buildings of the city were neat and orderly, the sky above was distant and deep blue.

'It's a lovely day,' Owen remarked, following my gaze. 'The day of the earthquake was rather like this, very blue and calm.'

I asked him if he could still remember the event clearly.

'Oh, absolutely. Very clear indeed. It was the first day of my second year at Napier Boys' High School. In the first week we always did military drill and so everybody was lined up on the flat field in front of the school. Just after eleven o'clock I heard this roaring sound and everything started shaking violently. The most astonishing thing was the ground. I can still see the way it rippled towards us like the waves of the sea. Then there was this enormous jolt that threw most people off their feet and that was followed by a swaying movement that went on for several minutes.'

'There must have been a moment when you had no idea what was happening?'

Owen paused. 'I suppose so. Nobody yelled out. In fact I don't think anyone said anything as far as I can remember. We must have been too shocked.

'I didn't fall over, but I remember looking up and seeing the huge hoarding that stood up from the roof of the two-storeyed administration block rocking in this alarming manner. Then out onto the steps through the main doors came "Potty" Foster, our diminutive headmaster. We called him Potty because he was round-shaped, you understand. I'll never forget it. He was wearing his flowing black gown and looked as if he was about to assert some authority over the calamity. Then the whole hoarding came crashing down on top of him. There was dust everywhere and I remember thinking that was the last we'd see of Potty.

'There was a long pause and then, covered in dust, Potty rose from the rubble like the phoenix and ran for his life towards the open field. He didn't look too much in command at that point.'

No one was aware of the devastation that was occurring in the rest of the town. A master told the boys to go home. On Marine Parade they saw smoke and flames and burst water pipes.

'As a boy of thirteen,' said Owen, grinning at the memory, 'I felt half excited and half apprehensive. I walked along Marine Parade and up Coote Road, which led to my home on the hill, just down from here, but I was stopped by a group of men and told to go and sit on the beach. I can still see people walking past in a sort of dazed state, one man with a string of sausages around his neck. I think he'd pinched them from the butcher's.

'Then someone hollered, "Oi, you lot, get off the beach, there could be a tidal wave." This time I wasn't stopped on Coote Road and I got to our big old two-storeyed house on Thompson Road. Did you see Thompson Road on the way up the hill? Well, our house was just beyond the water tower. All the chimneys were down and my mother's large supply of home-made preserves were smashed all over the floor and covered in soot. But the house was intact and we learnt later that all the family had survived.

'The next few weeks were a bit of an adventure to someone my age. We lived outside together with our neighbours. Luckily the weather was fine. We had no water because the water tower had collapsed and there was no electricity. Water was brought to us in a cart. We collected it in a bucket and cooked in the open on fires. There was no sewerage, of course, so we dug long-drops.

'Looking back, I realise I learnt a lot, not just how to cope physically but how not to judge by appearances. You see, all the divisions between people went out the window. Everyone pitched in and offered their skills and we were jolly glad to have them. I really found out what self-reliance means and I watched the amazing ability people have to get through a tragedy by working for everybody's good, not just their own.'

They were lessons undoubtedly put to good use when Owen found himself a prisoner of war for three-and-half years in Italy and Germany during World War II.

'I don't look on myself as anything special,' he said. 'Those sorts of things are just the experiences you have in your lifetime. If you survive them, you're lucky, that's all.'

Back in the caravan that evening the cellphone bleeped to announce Sue Wilson, my only niece, who lived with her husband near Frasertown at the back of Wairoa.

'Come up here for a few days,' she said. 'There's plenty of room and we'd love to see the caravan – and you of course.'

I started to say, 'Well, we're busy at the moment…' and then stopped. We weren't at all. There was nothing ahead of us. We were free to go wherever we wanted to whenever we wanted to – no meetings, no social engagements, no chores, no plans, nothing to hobble our nights and days. How odd.

'How about tomorrow?' I said.

'Fine. See you when we see you, then.'

Sue and Fenton Wilson lived with their two young children, Jonty and Alice, in a small comfortable house overlooking a valley of walnut trees. Fenton's shoulders, thick with muscle, attested to his time as a shearing contractor and in part accounted for his appointment as the emergency management officer for the district. He managed the family farm, 440 hectares of medium hill country, which carried about 1300 sheep and 220 cows. When Sue had married him and come to Frasertown a decade earlier she had already begun experimenting with preserves and now she had a thriving business making delightful combinations from oils and local produce and marketing them all around New Zealand.

When the caravan lumbered up the drive she abandoned for a moment the avalanche of capsicum and garlic she was preparing for pickling and came to the door to greet us.

'Man, it's hot,' she said, pushing her hair off her forehead with the back of her hand.

On the shelves in the small commercial kitchen were jars of salsas, fruit jellies, pickled walnuts, brandied cherries, flavoured coffee crystals, glacé orange rolls, lemons in gin and fruits in brandy, all awaiting labels.

The afternoon just got hotter and Sue took us with the children on a jaunt across a neighbouring farm for a dip in a river. It was here that I very nearly ended my life.

This river-of-no-name came from the hills and at one point narrowed to run in a natural gutter down the edge of a large, sloping rock bed. After about 12 metres it broke into a churning, rocky waterfall and crashed into a small lake. The bottom of the gutter had become covered in slimy weed to form a perfect natural waterslide. Who needed Water World?

I had not reckoned on the force of the water. What started out as a cruisy glide in an upright sitting position rapidly became an out-of-control freefall. I tipped onto my back and gathered momentum, my arms and legs waving in the air like those of a dying fly. And as I hurtled faster and faster towards a horrible demise, I caught a fleeting glimpse of my favourite niece and my beloved partner. They were doubled up with mirth.

A metre above the waterfall came my one chance of salvation in the form of a puny-looking branch sticking out from a small tree and stretched across the chute. If I could only get my feet high enough to push against it...I calculated, lifted my legs, and connected. It stopped me dead. I was home, but hardly dry, and there I had to remain inelegantly posed like an over-eager hooker until Bill could reach me. It seemed to take an age. Evidently it's not easy to clamber over slippery rocks when you are convulsing with laughter.

Country life, I decided, could throw up some very disconcerting experiences.

Of Cows and Cockroaches

We had a ring from a contact in Nelson who wanted a house painted in March. Bill had been putting feelers out around the country to see what work he could get . He was an exceptionally good painter. As well as being a perfectionist by nature, he'd had experience in the boat-building industry and built two houses of his own. In my opinion, anyone who got a 'Bill-job' got a bargain.

'So it looks like Nelson for a bit,' he said.

'That's fine by me.'

We had three weeks to get there and so we didn't have to race south. Half way down the island we ventured off the main route to stay with Andrew and Helen Gordon, about an hour's winding drive out into the steep hills towards the coast from Dannevirke. The pastureland on the drive to the farm was pocked with thistles and gouged with slips exposing grey-coloured clay. It was a distant spot close to a tiny country village called Pongaroa, and the couple lived in an old villa-style farmhouse, which they were gradually doing up. Single-handedly Andrew ran 656 hectares of remote high country where he had about 4000 Romney/Perendale sheep and 400 Angus cattle. He also had an area of radiata pine forest and, whenever he had time, he planted poplar and willows in the gullies to stabilise the hillside and stop further erosion.

The weather, which changed rapidly in these hills, turned turtle.

It was still warm but great inky clouds billowed over the tops and dumped steady soaking rain that lasted for three days and turned the ground to a spongy mush. The caravan's waterproofing was severely tested. It held up well enough except for a leak through the back window that soaked into my underwear drawer. And at night a regular drip just beside my head from a small guttering on the edge of the roof was like Chinese water torture. Bill rolled up a sliver of tinfoil and plugged the outlet – and this bit of Heath Robinson inventiveness was retained for two years.

Rain or not, Andrew rode his big bay gelding out to the back of the farm to bring in cows ready for scanning the next day. He looked like the man from Snowy River in his Driza-Bone with his dripping dogs trotting loyally after him. In the farmhouse we sat and drank tea and ate Helen's lemon muffins warm from the oven.

Bill and I discovered that we had some livestock of our own. Cockroaches had invaded the caravan. They were large and black and had a habit of dropping down out of nowhere with a soft plunk. One night one landed on my pillow. I flicked the undesirable bed-mate onto the floor and jumped on it and then bullied Bill out of bed to up-end and examine every bit of bedding.

Next morning we were woken at first light as the huge gathering of cattle was driven past us down the road to the yards. Their moaning, screeching protest sounded like a chorus from the depths of Hades. Maybe they knew what they were in for. Scanning was an extremely undignified process that involves the insertion of a long probe. If a cow was not pregnant she was considered of no further use and that was the end of her. She never returned to greener grass. I decided I would do everything I could not to come back to earth as a cow or a cockroach.

The next mob of anything that we encountered was a few days later, close to Hunterville. We were parked just off the road having lunch, when a mob of a couple of thousand sheep trundled through. It took half an hour for them to pass but, unlike Andrew's cows, they travelled without raising hell.

It turned out that a few days spent in Hunterville also gave me the chance to meet a particularly fascinating man. On the main road into town was an attractive little white stucco cottage that looked as if it should be placed somewhere in the south of Ireland. I mentioned it to Susanna Grace, a local woman who'd invited me to tea. We were sitting under an oak tree in the very grand garden that she and her husband had created on their property close to the town.

'Oh, that belongs to the bear man,' she said. 'You know, the guy that goes off and saves bears in Pakistan or wherever.'

'You mean Peter Henderson? *That* bear man?'

'That's him. Do you want to meet him? I can give him ring if you want.'

Within half an hour I was talking to a tall, handsome, fit-looking New Zealander who told me he had an appointment for a hair cut in an hour and the next day was off to Auckland to catch a plane to Pakistan.

I got straight to the point. 'Was it something you'd planned to do – to save bears?'

'Not in my wildest dreams,' he said. 'It's something I sleep-walked into. You see, when my marriage broke up and my wife returned to England taking one of our children with her, I followed with my two other daughters to try to reconcile the marriage. Unfortunately, that didn't work out. For a while I managed farms in Hampshire and then I was offered a contract job in Turkey to help erect electric fencing for the World Society for the Protection of Animals on a project that was being set up to rescue dancing bears. In India and Pakistan alone there are a couple of thousand dancing bears and fifty fighting bears in need of rescue.

'I've been working for WSPA for five years now,' Peter went on. 'In Pakistan, Romania, Bulgaria and Turkey, Hungary and Ecuador, and what I've done is to help set up sanctuaries and then encourage the owners to release their bears to them. It has not been a simple process. Wherever I find a bear in trouble there is a people problem to go with it – a morass of political incompetence, bureaucracy and corruption. In the Punjab, for instance, bear-dog fights are illegal but the police won't do anything because rich and influential friends are involved.'

I was full of admiration for his work and said so.

'I don't want you to think I'm an animal-hugging extremist sort of person,' he said with some force. 'I don't hold with that sort of thing. I think with my head – not my heart. Being practical enables me to do the job.'

Peter went to another room and brought out a collection of photographs. He pointed to one of a fight, taken from the air. It was in a village in southern Pakistan. A bear and a dog were attacking each other in a bare, dusty arena, around which stood a huge crowd of onlookers. The image was so grotesque I found it hard to look at. In amongst the throng were figures that were clearly identifiable as police. Outside of the circle were several more bears.

'Some of those are dead,' Peter told me. 'You can see for yourself that the law of land is clearly being flouted. Well, I took this photograph to the authorities as proof of what is happening. They did nothing.'

He shuffled though the pile and brought out photographs of the project he had spearheaded in Pakistan. They showed a 5-hectare enclosure, which had small square caves built into the brick wall around it, and a central water trough.

'It's not much,' he said, 'but it's a bear palace compared to the cramped little cages and hideously cruel treatment that many of the inmates have endured since the day they were born.'

'How do the locals feel about what you are doing?' I said.

'Pretty good in the main. I mean we don't just try to help the animals. There are plenty of spin-offs for the locals too. Twenty people were employed to help build that sanctuary you've just looked at and we injected about thirty thousand New Zealand dollars into their community. In other places we've worked on projects like providing clean water or toilets or helping with crops.

'I really want people to understand that nothing's perfect in these countries. All I aim to do is to take on a project and leave the animals in a better condition than when I found them. Each situation is so complex that I am happy with any progress. There are disappointments but the successes outweigh them.'

He stood up and looked at his watch. 'Anyway, I've talked too much. It's a bit of a pet subject at the moment. I'd better get off for that hair cut.'

On the day Peter left for Pakistan we left for the Kapiti Coast, which didn't have quite the same ring to it. I wondered how I'd get by in Pakistan living in a tent and rescuing bears. Honourable, I thought, but decidedly dodgy.

On the coast we parked at a camping ground close to the beach. It was in dismal shape – the ablution block was worse than basic, no hot water, no water attachments for the caravan, no television reception and drinking water available only from a small tank in the kitchen building. We were the only residents except for a couple with a van who pulled in late at night and left early – probably without paying.

Our reason for being there at all was to get onto Kapiti Island but we were told that we'd have to have booked about two weeks in advance at that time of the year. So we had to be content with a morning walk along a stretch of the grey sand that fringes this entire coastline. The trunks of dead trees had found their way ashore and their bleached shapes stuck up from the sand, appearing in the misty light like gatherings of ghosts. In reality there was nobody else on the beach except a Maori family gathering shellfish.

Seen from that angle Kapiti Island was the shape of a bell skirt and, in the early morning, it wore a frill of fog around its hemline. The sea was softly grey and puckered with little waves. The day was calm but trees bending inland indicated the unpredictable nature of this coast where, on the 24th of June, 1878, the square-rigged sailing ship *Hydrabad* was driven onto the sand.

We walked until we'd located the wreck, which we almost missed among the driftwood. All that remained were the rusting prow and the ribs of her iron hull, picked clean and poking out of the sand like the skeleton of a giant seagull. It took a lot of imagination to reconstruct her into a three-masted sailing ship, nearly 70 metres in length and fitted with carved teak panels, ornate cabin lamps and engraved silverware. At the time of her wreck she'd been sailing from Lyttelton to Adelaide with a full cargo of rolling stock and locomotive parts on board. A gale had pushed her hard onto the beach from which she stubbornly refused to be moved despite two attempts to salvage her.

Our next encounter with a ship would be with the ferry across Cook Strait, The Lynx. It was heavily booked at that time of the year and we had to find something else to do for seven days. We parked at Tatum Park, just south of Levin, in a paddock between the railway line and the road. It was far from restful but its outstanding advantage in weather that was extremely hot was that it had a swimming pool and mature trees. Sitting under an apple tree tipping water over my head to keep cool and flapping at the persistent flies that sought my company reminded me of being in Africa.

I went for walks along the railway line and put my ear to the track to see if I could hear the distant thunder of a train. It always worked in Western movies, but all I heard was my own heart thumping in my ear. In the evening, even at the height of summer, the track was cool. I wouldn't recommend the practice in winter. Kneeling with your backside pointing skyward and one ear iced to a railway track would be pushing the ridiculous.

Valentine's Day came up and we vacillated about whether to make a romantic fuss or let it go. We settled on a take-away Chinese meal from Simon's Café in Levin, which we ate sitting on the grass under an inky sky thick with stars. Then we drank the bottle of Moët et Chandon that we'd saved for over a year, and went tipsily to bed.

The only holiday park near Wellington was in the middle of an industrial area in Petone. It was well appointed, large and impersonal. At about four o'clock every afternoon the campervans, caravans, cars full of campers, cyclists with their tiny tents and the cabin renters started pouring in and there was a frenzy of setting up.

An older French couple carefully placed their national flag on the ridge of their tent with a flourish worthy of the fairy at the top of a Christmas tree. They were having *un temps formidable en Nouvelle Zélande*. I think that's what they told me – my French was no better than their English. Two much younger Norwegian girls with white hair, ropy leg muscles and ample floppy breasts had their country's flags blazoned across their T-shirts. This canvas set gathered in the kitchen in the evening, to cook and swap stories in their many languages about the events of their journeys.

We were more the mobile-home set. Alongside us a smoothly groomed German couple in a campervan pulled up and began their setting-up ritual. Ingrid was most unhappy. 'Eet eez hoopless,' she said. 'Da room is sooo small.' Most of the space in the van was taken up with two enormous suitcases. Her husband looked equally grumpy but said nothing.

In the morning there was frantic activity in the camping ground. The showers did overtime, the communal bathrooms smelt steamily of a mixture of soap, shampoo, deodorant and toothpaste. In tents and caravans, bowls of cereal were consumed, gear was checked and packed, hoses, television aerials and electrical cords disconnected, water containers filled, effluent dumped and, by nine-thirty, most of our nightly companions had left. In this place our social connections were fleeting and we seldom came across the same people twice.

We spent the days reading and visiting friends in the city. Bill played golf and I found some subjects to write magazine articles about. It was during this time in Petone that I made a discovery about an aspect of life I had never considered before. It was on a Sunday. Streaks of rose-coloured clouds heralded another still, hot day and I decided to walk before the sun's temper sent me scuttling into the shade. There was nowhere that offered beauty in the vicinity. The camp abutted an industrial area on one side and a trotting track on the other. I chose the industrial strip, where I thought I might at least reach the water at the edge of the bay.

The place was deserted and strangely eerie, as if the end of the world had come and I had been left behind. A loose piece of tin flapped against a wall of concrete. My spine tingled and I increased my walk rate, propelled partly by fear of the emptiness and partly by curiosity. Without the distraction of human company I was able to ponder the place around me. It was a world I had paid very little attention to in the past – the almost palpable testosterone-laden domain of boots and boiler suits and Swannies, of men striding about with authority doing men's business in men-speak.

I began to consider the purpose of galvanising plants, battery manufacturers, water techs, integrated logistics, metal art, paint production, industrial coatings, chrome plating, coiled springs for motor vehicles, steel tubes and die casting. What did all these things do? I mostly came up with a blank and the recognition of my ignorance intrigued me. How could I have lived so long in the world with such a rudimentary understanding of man-made construction?

The buildings where this production occurred were also masculine – bulky, square and muscular and made of concrete or steel or corrugated iron with no frills, little colour and few decorative embellishments apart from rust and barbed wire. And there was no seduction in the signage: 'Visitors report to office'; 'No smoking on site'; 'Delivery here'; 'We have moved'; 'No admittance'; 'Warning'.

And then, among all this, was a neat, brightly painted sign at the road edge which read, 'Quarry Inn. A business doing pleasure. Massage parlour and bar. Open 9 am till late.' I ventured down the drive and at the end was a plain two-storeyed house, painted white with lace curtains drawn across the windows. There was a large parking area at the back of it but on this day of rest it was empty. By the door of the house was another sign. 'Fully licensed house of ladies,' I read. 'Upmarket and intimate. One hour $130. Half hour $100. Twenty minutes $90. Cash prices.'

I returned to the caravan feeling bemused but slightly more educated in the ways of men.

Across the Water

Two days later Bill and I caught the early-morning ferry and, when the caravan and cars were safely stowed in the belly of The Lynx, we moved to comfortable seats in the bow of the boat where we could see where we were headed. As we slid out from the dock the motorway into Wellington was jammed with commuters, strung out in a necklace at the foot of the hills. The surface of the harbour was like billowing grey crimplene and the sky was mottled with high cloud.

There was no sign of the dolphins we had seen the day before. We'd been out on the sea with Bill's old sailing mate Bruce Green and his partner Caroline. In the past Greeny and Bill had crewed together on a yacht in Melbourne.

Close to Somes Island we had spotted a pod of dolphins and then another and another, until it seemed that the whole bay was flecked with movement. There must have been hundreds of them, maybe thousands. In the distance they looked like leaping sand fleas, closer in they took on the grace of ballet dancers as they sliced silkily through the water. One or two came up to the yacht, huffing in small explosions as they humped out of the water and then skimmed under the bow. At first they were travelling in all directions; after an hour or more, perhaps in response to some cetaceous signal, they turned and started undulating towards the heads and the open sea. They were a marvellous sight.

Today as The Lynx moved out through the heads her bow began to dip rhythmically into a well-defined swell. We sat in comfort in the lounge sipping lattes and I thought about the crossings I used to make four times a year when I was a student in Dunedin. Then we'd travelled overnight to Lyttelton on the *Rangatira* or the *Maori* and held parties in the forward cabin until everyone became too seasick to continue. In the morning we'd flirt with the stewards at breakfast, longing for shipboard romances over our dreadful coffee and hot pies – even if they only lasted for a few hours.

A man came and dumped himself down in the seat next to me. A pronounced beer belly forced him to leave his jacket unzipped and, even though we were inside, a woollen hat perched on the back of his head. One of his eyes was covered by a thick white surgical swab.

'The name's Steve, from Taranaki. Bloody hell, it's as big as a bloody hay barn in here,' he said, looking around the enclosed foredeck. And then confidingly: 'Dunno why I'm going to the South Island anyway; it's perfectly good back home.'

'That's a rather one-eyed point of view,' said Bill.

Steve didn't get it. 'Yeah,' he said uncertainly.

A mollymawk, great wings outstretched, wheeled close to the window of the ferry and then we slid into a sea fog and the seascape whited out. I was always mesmerised by the sea – from its endless sloppy movement to its awesome potential. But there was nothing to see in a fog. I dug my book out of my rucksack. *Passage to Juneau* by Jonathan Raban was about a rather longer sea journey in which the author sailed the Inside Passage from Seattle, Washington, to Juneau, Alaska. I read a passage about the sea which was breathtaking in its precision.

I fear the bushfire crackle of the breaking wave as it topples into foam; the inward suck of the tidal whirlpool; the loom of a big ocean swell, sinister and dark, in windless calm; the rip, the eddy, the race; the sheer abyssal depth of the water, as one floats like a trustful beetle on the surface tension.

I was happy that, apart from this crossing, our own journey was on terra firma. I was no sea-gypsy.

In the seat behind me a young man was ringing his friend in Nelson. 'Is that Maria?' he said into his cellphone. 'I'll be there soon, sweetie possum. I'm on the ferry and I'm heading south.'

This was a common misconception. Once through Pencarrow and Sinclair Heads, which marked the exit of Wellington Harbour, the route to Tory Channel and Picton was not south but west and slightly north, turning to the south-west in Queen Charlotte Sound. Not that I could claim a great sense of direction. I'd often enough made the same mistake as sweetie possum's man.

As we neared the cliffs of Arapawa Island and made the turn into Tory Channel the volume of the ferry's music system was suddenly increased, perhaps to evoke the drama of arrival. I was astonished to hear not the lilting softness of an appropriate Maori greeting song, but the melody of what was unmistakably 'Sweet Leilani'. And so we were welcomed into the arms of the South Island to the plaintive twang of Hawaiian guitars.

Apart from the music, our arrival in the South Island was without ceremony. In the protection of Queen Charlotte Sound, the deep, slow-moving water was green like textured glass, so unruffled in the scalloped little bays that the pine trees that darkened the hills were reflected perfectly in its surface. The boat slowed from its cruising speed of 40 knots to half speed to diminish the disturbance that its wake brought to the shoreline, and half an hour later we docked smoothly and silently at the Picton Wharf.

For a reason that was never explained, the ferry was running late and we had been ordered to be ready for rapid disembarking.

I was at the front of the line-up and as we docked I was sitting in the car with my hand poised dutifully over the keys.

'You'll be off first,' said a traffic controller who wore a creaking leather jacket and dangling dreadlocks that looked as if they had been dipped in cow dung. 'Just wait 'ntil I tell you to go.' It flashed through my mind that if he didn't have his timing right I could hurtle from the bowels of the catamaran and nose-dive ignominiously into the sea.

Safely delivered to the wharf a few moments later, I adjusted the wing mirror to watch Bill's progress. Behind the Safari the caravan swayed off the ship with the shambling grace of a sashaying elephant. It was nudged along by the stream of vehicles behind it and for a while the landing buzzed with a bee swarm of activity. Half an hour later, it was almost deserted.

We made our way to the Blue Anchor Holiday Park on Waikawa Road and squeezed the caravan in beside that of Sam and his wife Mary. They were in their late seventies and came from Hamilton. They'd left two years earlier for a three-month caravan tour of the South Island and they had never gone home.

'It's great in the south,' Sam assured me. 'Never been here before so I didn't know what I was missing till we got here.'

He showed us a portfolio of the wood-turned furniture he once made for a living and explained how now he used his skills to repair bits and pieces at the various camping grounds they travelled to. He said that he was much in demand and by bartering camping fees for work the two of them got by quite nicely.

'Do you have thoughts of going home?' I said.

'Nope. No way. Why would we? Not until we can think of a reason.'

I liked the sound of that and when we waved them goodbye next day I felt cheerfully bold about life on the road. Maybe we'd never go home either.

. . .

The route to Nelson along the edge of the Sounds was a treat. Queen Charlotte Drive turned off to the right in the centre of town and the road wound sharply uphill. From the top of the rise there was an eagle-eye view back over the town and the harbour. To Katherine Mansfield the houses on the hills looked like 'shells on the lid of a box'. I thought they didn't look much different now, although there must have been a lot more of them.

For the next 35 kilometres the road swung along bushy hillsides that rose straight from the water's edge. Occasionally it snaked down to small, indented bays with clusters of colourful holiday houses squeezed in between the water and the hills. The bits that dipped and turned like a roller-coaster afforded excellent views of mountain spurs and labyrinths of rich green water, but it would have been too easy to end up as part of the scenery if we'd taken our eyes off the road.

At the swampy toe of Pelorus Sound we pulled up in the centre of Havelock. The old wooden buildings of this fishing hamlet had been retained and many of them tarted up and put to good use as museums, antique or craft shops and restaurants. Much of the Sounds' huge harvest of green mussels passed through Havelock on its way to be processed and shipped to overseas markets. We called in to the Mussel Boys restaurant in the main street and ate a plate of 'flats' with a glass of Guinness. When we wanted coffee the waitress directed us across the road to the Darling Dill Café.

'We don't do coffee,' she said, quaintly.

About 150 years earlier Havelock's prosperity had been forged from the gold rush. There were twenty-three breweries in town and innumerable distilleries thriving in the bush. Now there appeared to be only one distillery. It belonged to Ruffy, who had a large wooden whisky-bottle-shaped letterbox at his gate. The label advertised his product – obviously not for sale. I would have liked a taste of Ruffy's whisky but I knocked on the door and Ruffy wasn't home.

In the old gold days the lifestyle in Havelock did little to honour the extensive credentials of the man after whom the town was named: 'Sir Henry Havelock, distinguished commander-in-chief of the British Forces in India, triumphant in the relief of Cawnpore and the defence of Lucknow during the Indian Mutiny.' But the town had two illustrious sons of its own. Ernest Rutherford was a giant of physics and split the atom and engineer William Pickering was a doyen among space scientists. We peeked inside the little wooden school they attended in the main street, which was now a youth hostel.

We continued west through Mt Richmond Forest Park, and much of the drive was past exotic forests. When we stopped to check if the caravan was still properly coupled to the truck I laid a complaint.

'I'm no fan of all these regiments of pinus radiata,' I said.

'I quite like them,' Bill said. 'They're attractive in their own way.'

I could concede that where the trees were still standing they had a dark, foreign kind of beauty. But the harvested areas, with dead branches lying about like spilt matches, offended me. If such utter devastation was necessary to harvest the timber then I wished I didn't have to look at it.

The last leg of the drive wound up over the Whangamoa Saddle and was mantled with foliage until it dipped towards the ocean and we had the first breathtaking glimpse of the wide steel-blue stretch of Tasman Bay. My sense of well-being matched the view. I'd been driving behind Bill because I wanted to see how much black smoke the Safari blew on the steep climbs – not too bad. But now I passed him and waved. He gave me the thumbs up.

Commit Merriment

We found our way to Nelson's Tahuna Beach Holiday Park at Tahunanui. It was later to gain infamy as the venue for the New Year's party from hell but at that time it was quiet and respectable.

We chose a site on a small flat-topped hill surrounded by poplar trees that were beginning to shed their papery leaves. They fluttered about like fairies before settling on the ground as a gentle reminder that winter was on its way. We were going to be there for six weeks or more and so we dickered with our position on the site as if we were building a five-star apartment. Where did we want the sun to be in morning? Where should the door be? Which way should the awning open? Where would we park the cars? It was dark by the time we had finished.

The next day Bill started his house painting and I was left behind like a regular housewife – with no house. On a practical level, freedom by way of a caravan was very confined. At first this was hell for an untidy mind. Everything had to be put away in its exact spot as soon as we had finished with it. But I came to like this as well as the strait-jacket routine that brought life to order.

Every morning Bill got up, opened the vent, made the tea, organised the porridge and went for a shower. Then I got up and dressed, made the bed, cooked the porridge and, when Bill returned, left him space in the caravan to eat breakfast and get organised and went to empty the water bucket, roll up the windows and go for a shower.

By the time I got back Bill was ready to leave for work. I waved him off, ate my own breakfast and did the dishes and then busied myself like Mrs Tittlemouse, fussing through the cupboards, dusting the window frames, wiping the windows of condensation, cleaning the hob and fridge and pegging out the washing. I could spring-clean in half an hour and reach the microwave with my right hand the same time I was changing the television station with my left. Admittedly, I spent a lot of time on my knees scrabbling around in inadequate cupboards but with our no-frills lifestyle the inconvenience was not an issue – not yet. We'd stripped the number of clothes, utensils and books we had down to bare essentials and I didn't miss a thing. I thought of all the paraphernalia I had at home and I couldn't remember what I'd done with it.

Getting organised for the day, even if I spun it out, only took me an hour-and-a-half and, with nothing left to do, I was forced to turn to the business of earning a living. There was plenty to write about in Nelson. Over the years it had attracted not only serious artists, artisans and craftspeople, but also innovative entrepreneurs who were decidedly outside the square.

In the two months we were there I found bone carvers, knife makers, wood sculptors, steel artists, glass blowers, potters, clay sculptors, jewellers, furniture makers, textile artists, cartoonists, song writers and musicians, but I certainly didn't find them all. There were about 400 people in the region whose occupation was documented as 'artist'.

I couldn't fathom exactly what had encouraged the creative, experimental side of Nelson. The open beauty of the environment had something to do with it, and the long hours of sunshine, but there were other places with those qualities and they hadn't attracted quite the same gatherings of talent and aptitude. Maybe it was a hangover from the early settlers who found their freedom there and tried to express how good it felt in any way they could. Whatever the reason, more and more people seemed to be breaking loose from lives that had been too long tethered by convention and settling in Nelson. They came from Germany, the United Kingdom and America as much as they did from Auckland, Wellington and Christchurch.

There was a definite twinkle to life in Nelson that I sometimes found missing in other parts of provincial New Zealand. Who but a wag, for instance, would call a popular bar in town the Pheasant Plucker in the Bush (a terrible trap for malaprops); or paint a sign for the road meandering around the shoreline of the peninsula suburb of Monaco that read 'Be very careful, old biddies and rug rats all over the road'; or plant a notice on their letterbox announcing 'No bills thanks – can't pay them'; or put a sign at the front of their bus that said 'No eating. No drinking. No messing around.'

Other types of twinkle were nothing short of wacky. From advertisements in local newspapers and community noticeboards I was informed that I had just missed the full moon gathering of drumming and fine art, but the possibility of learning how to cultivate a body of nectar from the master teacher Virochana of Colorado was still a go, and I could also meet with Wild Women and Weeds, who would help me explore the tradition of healing rituals, or I could learn aspects of kriya, tantra and eternal yoga, essential to attaining ascension.

There were many people in Nelson who didn't merely pay lip service to doing their own thing. As well as all that art and cosmic exploration the area supported the sort of individualistic pursuits that no one could exactly call art but were still of a highly creative nature. One afternoon when I didn't have much else to do – which was frequently – I went to see a man in Mapua who was a good illustration of this phenomenon.

Sir Greg was the owner and director of the Station Museum in the main street of the village. The building was an old Nissen hut to which had been added a red-and-white facade. A small model of an old biplane perched on the hoarding. Initially this building had been the headquarters of the Fort Custard Fire Department Theatrical Company. Now it housed Greg's extensive collection of military uniforms and paraphernalia. He had more than 200 uniforms – some for hire and others for display. He was also an actor and, even as I was introducing myself, I nailed him as Captain Mainwaring from *Dad's Army*. This was the stage persona he was best known for and, even out of uniform, there was an uncanny resemblance – the same height and portliness, the same round face and a way of talking in abbreviated sentences with a kind of boxed-in energy.

He looked up from the soft-peaked khaki hat he was putting finishing touches to and beamed.

'Gidday,' he said in a distinctly Kiwi greeting. 'I'll just glue this and I'll be right with you. This is for a uniform from the Mounted Rifles, New Zealand Army, First World War.' He applied the glue to a bit of lining and held it tightly between his thumb and forefinger. 'I've got some really rare ones. Come 'n' look at this. It belonged to a colonel from the Russian Red Guard. It's even got fifteen original medals.' Then he pointed to a handsome, bright red jacket with black collar and cuffs. 'This is a New Zealand Queen's Volunteer jacket from the Maori wars.'

Greg's acting skills were self-taught. He was well known locally but came to national notice with his depiction of Captain Mainwaring in a skit from *Dad's Army* for Warbirds over Wanaka. Now he was also known as Warrant Officer Warwick, René from *Allo Allo* and a multitude of other characters that he worked in to his theatrical burlesques. He hired himself out, sometimes on his own and sometimes with other actors, for performances and skits around the South Island.

I asked him about his fascination with war, which had some of the hallmarks of obsession.

'Yeah, well it is a bit, but it's the theatre of it,' he said, 'not the killing. I like the drama, the costuming, the pomp and ceremony. As a kid I used to sit in the car drinking raspberry juice outside the local RSA while my dad met up with his war mates.

'When I got older I was allowed to sit on the steps and watch military films. Some of the men yarned about the wars they'd been in, others gave me old tokens such as hats and badges. They turned out to be the start of my collection.'

He pointed to a complete New Zealand Volunteers uniform from the Boer War. 'One of the old blokes gave me that when I was eleven,' he said. 'Much later I found out that people were really interested in uniforms of all kinds and so I bought myself a shelf full of uniform books and taught myself to sew.'

Being with Greg was a bit like spending time at the theatre. He slipped in and out of the persona of the character he was talking about and sometimes, I think, forgot that I was there. On the first Sunday of every month he fired a military cannon from the wharf – just because it was Sunday. 'Some people think all their Sundays have come at once,' he confided with a Mainwaring twinkle.

Some of Greg's self-training was in the Mapua Leisure Park across the road, where he was the entertainment officer. The park was another example of Nelson's *je ne sais quoi*. Bill and I didn't get our gear off but if you wanted to it was all part of the fun. You could sit in a section of the camp there and be surrounded by fellow campers nonchalantly striding around in the altogether. The trick was not to turn a hair at any of the astonishing sights that might wander past. Despite gyms, diets and cosmetic surgery, God's infinite variety when he designed the human frame was in evidence.

. . .

A man who intrigued me almost as much as Sir Greg was Steve Richards, who lived not far down the road from him, on the way to Motueka. He and his wife Judy had a restaurant called Jester House, which was well known around those parts.

I parked in the shade of a large tree and then footed it across a small bridge over a stream full of large eels that came slithering up out of the water to snatch at hand-offered morsels. I watched other people risk their fingers. Not mine – I'd gained a healthy respect for eels when I was bitten by a large one my father had caught and hung up by the tail. I was about ten years old and I shoved my finger in its mouth to see if it was still alive. It avenged itself on my unsuspecting digit.

At the entrance to Jester House just before the bridge was a notice written in bold, black letters: 'COMMIT MERRIMENT'. I walked around an old wooden villa, which was the restaurant, and through a garden full of curious bits and pieces that looked a bit like something out of Dr Seuss – wonky wooden chairs, a person-sized chess set, a giant toaster, a tiger effigy peering out from the bushes, a maze and various sculptures including one of a voluptuous female strumming a guitar, bearing the caption 'Rockin' Mama'. Behind this garden was another more orderly one that wrapped around the couple's own house. The house was home-made of rammed earth and large wooden beams. It looked lived-in and well loved and somehow off-centre, although I couldn't quite work out why I thought that.

Judy and Steve were having a day off from the restaurant. They were grubbing around in a patch of earth next to their latest zany venture, a two-storeyed building shaped like a giant boot – complete with laces. Considering I had just pitched up there the two of them were very welcoming.

'Don't let me stop you working,' I said.

'No, no,' they protested, plucking off their gardening gloves. 'We're ready for a break.'

'Where's the old woman?' I said, waving a hand in the direction of the boot.

'Aha,' said Steven, who was a long lanky creature with half a head of red hair. 'That's our new accommodation and it's not for old women or children. It's for couples who want a romantic weekend.'

We sat in the sun on the verandah of the house and for a while talked about restaurants and food and dealing with customers. Judy, who was tall with blonde hair pulled back off her face, seemed slightly jaded with the demands of the restaurant but I could've struck her on a bad day.

'You know you two've got a bit of reputation for being different,' I said to Steve.

'That's easy enough to get,' he said. 'People probably think you're pretty different too – living in a caravan.

'I guess so. It doesn't feel like that to us.'

'Exactly. Quite frankly, anything we do feels pretty normal to us. We just want to be happy, same as everybody else and for me that means good food, great surroundings and lots of socialising. If anything is worth doing I reckon it's worth having fun doing it, so I dress up in weird clothes to help set the tone. We don't feel at all constrained by convention. We can do what we want as long as it doesn't hurt anyone.'

Steve and Judy met when they both belonged to Alf's Imperial Army. The prototype for the Imperial Army was the invention of Christchurch's Wizard who, concerned at the lack of innocent fun for young people, ran several humorous events known as giant stirs. On these, excitement was built to a crescendo and then released in an energetic orgy of harmless activity. As far as I could work out it mostly involved throwing flour bombs at an opposing force in mock warfare.

'In 1984, during one of our battles,' said Steve, 'I was captured by the opposition, and that day it was the McGillicuddy Serious

Party. A witch put a spell on me and I had to stay. I couldn't go back to Alf's Army.' All of this might have started to sound like a story by CS Lewis, except that Steve told it as if it were an account of the Vietnam War. Nothing in his face expressed a lack of gravity.

'Jester House is the Tasman headquarters for the McGillicuddy Party,' he said, 'only there isn't a party any more. It's been disbanded and we only have clan meetings now. We're regressionalists who see the possibility for a better way of life and that's why we called our central policy the Great Leap Backwards. Our election promises were to burn the Beehive, abolish Parliament and sack all MPs. We were going to ban electricity, outlaw money and ship all modern technology overseas to pay off debts, and then set up a nationwide network of semi-autonomous clans and tribes. We believe, you see, that humans are social forest-edge dwellers – just a bunch of primates really. And the McGillicuddy Party was a group of environmental, socialist funnists – so green it was yellow because there was no blue…'

And there we had to leave it. Judy was entertaining friends for lunch and had already delivered two pizzas to a setting under the large sun umbrella in the garden. Steve had been called to the pleasures of the table.

I drove to Rabbit Island and sat down on the beach to eat my own lunch – a tomato sandwich and a bunch of grapes – and I watched the flannel-grey waves flopping against the stones and thought about the implications of life as a fringe-dwelling primate.

Degrees of Dislocation

Every Saturday a lot of the divergent talent of Nelson gathered in Montgomery Square in the centre of the city to try their luck at the market. I considered myself to be a highly developed market connoisseur and to me the Nelson market was one of the most exuberant in the country. Going there every Saturday morning became a habit.

I went not just to look at the coloured socks and outlandish hats, hand-crafted possum slippers, crystal mobiles, bizarre jewellery, animal doorstops, polished paua shells, baby bibs or ancient essences. Nor did I go to taste the mussels and whitebait fritters or to eat the cheeses, breads, vegie pies and spicy Dutch doughnuts or drink the organic coffee and super smoothies. I went there to listen to the pan piper, the drummers, the violin player and the sword player, and because there was an essential Nelson-ness about the gathering: the ingenious creations, the tolerance of the quirky and curious, the vendors' spirit of generosity and the boisterous good humour of the crowd.

On Sundays the flea market was held at the same venue. This was quite a different gathering where second-hand clothing and collected bric-a-brac was sold from the ground or the boots of cars. As each car arrived and opened its boot a crowd gathered around and rummaged through the offerings, holding sad little items aloft and haggling over the price. There was an air of desperation at the Sunday market that was quite absent on Saturdays.

I watched a man in a worn leather jacket and sandalled feet elbow his way through a group of bargain hunters and grab a bedside lamp, which he thrust above his head.

'Two dollars for this,' he called in a gruff voice.

The sales woman was dressed in a loose purple top and a long velvet skirt. Her feet were bare. 'Two fifty.'

'Two twenty-five.'

She shrugged and the deal was struck.

Later I wandered to the other end of the market and there was the same man with a table set up beside his dust-caked pick-up. On it was the lamp wearing a price tag of $4.50.

In the Nelson camping ground we had moved off the main road of suburbia into a pocket of the world that had its own rules, rhythms and meanings, and it was there that I felt I was really getting the hang of this caravanning thing.

In the awning I'd set up a folding bed (for visitors should they arrive), books, buckets and golf bags and the fold-away clothes horse we used in wet weather. Our shoes and boots went in a box under the bed and in another were my books and spare office equipment. If it was raining the awning was a buffer zone from outside to inside. Although the floor by the entrance, which was through a flap of canvas, got oozy with mud in the wet, it was better than having mud glued to the caravan floor. Like everybody else we clumped around outside in gumboots when it was wet and changed them for slippers when we went indoors.

We were there long enough to have moved up the hierarchy of campsite life to become 'semis'. The 'permanents' had a certain status, a kind of silently acknowledged proprietorial claim to the place. I felt closer to the permanents being a semi. Permanents

stayed in a section of the grounds that was roped off from the rest
of us. They put down roots in their little gardens and marked off
their territory with shade cloth or picket fencing. Some had solid
awnings that enlarged their living spaces.

Joanna was a permie. We got chatting in the laundry and I liked
her immediately. She had the stature of a cushion and an open
face that shone with contentment and the effects of a healthy
lifestyle. She told me that you couldn't afford to be worried about
status symbols if you lived in a caravan park.

'Living like we do is considered to be not quite proper,' she
grinned. 'Some people seem to think we're all on the dole and
living rough. It's rubbish, of course. You'd have to say the
architecture is nothing special and I s'pose we're all pretty low-
budget, but most of us have got a real rich attitude to life.

'This is not just a stopping place between adventures for us. Me
and my hubby have been here two years now – on the road four
years before that. We've got everything we want, close to the beach,
plenty of sunshine, a cosy place to live with all the mod cons and
good company when we want it. Where else can you get all that
for next to nothing, eh? We don't have to socialise unless we choose
to and we're allowed our personal twitches without people wanting
us to be like everybody else.'

Joanna and her husband were going to move on one day soon.
'We think we'll try things in Oz,' she said. 'There are some great
camping grounds there, right on the sea.'

I talked to Marion Nelson sometimes too. She and her husband
had come to the Tahuna camp from Blenheim nine years earlier.
They had set up their caravan and added a rigid awning and floor
to create a sitting room. Then they erected a fence and developed
a small garden, which was neatly stuffed with healthily growing
ferns and bright flowers, a bird bath and a small fish pond. Under
a pergola in one corner was a wooden platform with a barbecue
and a comfortable table and chairs.

'Gerry loves cooking out here when we entertain,' she told me. 'It's his special place.' There was also room for a small tin shed where Gerry distilled whisky as a hobby, and next to it a hot-house covered in plastic where Marion germinated plants.

The first time I met Marion she was packing all her worldly goods into boxes and it looked as if she was moving out.

'Not a chance,' she said. 'They'll carry *me* out in a box. I love it here. I can't think of a better lifestyle.'

She was a sturdy, grey-haired, practical woman, her hands roughened by work, her face enlivened by a puckish sense of humour. She chuckled sheepishly as she told me how she'd left the stew on the stove the other morning and had gone off to work. By the time she'd remembered it was almost too late. Smoke was curling through the caravan and awning and had already damaged the interior. She was packing things away so that it could be relined.

'When we came here it was fine for a while when we were setting up,' she said. 'And then I got bored and said to the manager, "If you've got any gardening you want done, I'll do it." He was happy enough about that. Then, when I'd been doing the gardens a while for nothing, I said to him, "I think we need to talk about this." That's how I became the paid gardener and now I'm anything. I make curtains for the cabins, mind the shop when the manager needs a break and organise a lot of the functions in the entertainment hall. It's all great fun and keeps me flat out.'

Now that it was late autumn we had plenty of room between us and our nearest neighbour in the park. John, who lived in a bus, was also a semi. There were unspoken rules among semis. We didn't visit each other's homes but migrated to a kind of a 'chat spot' where we exchanged information. There was very little probing as to who we were, where we came from, why we were on the road or how we earned a living. I liked that – but I still managed to winkle out a little about our neighbours without seeming to pry.

John was a big, bearded solitary man with long hair and the

little of his face that was visible was crumpled like brown paper. A roll-your-own sucked to the butt balanced permanently on the corner of his lower lip. It hung there even when he laughed. He had been on the road for seven years and had a temporary job working on the fishing boats.

'But I try not to work,' he said. 'I don't need the stress. When I needs money I buys an old motorbike, gets it in running order and sells it for a bit of a profit.' He looked at our caravan and awning, at the Safari and Bill's aged but polished Merc. 'You must be loaded,' he said without a hint of envy.

Another neighbour was Neville, who disappeared into his caravan every Friday night with a six-pack under his arm, drew the curtains and didn't seem to emerge until Monday, when he drove off noisily in his rusty blue Falcon well before I had got my first eyelid open. I invented a murky past for Neville but, when I finally ambushed him on the way to the toilet one evening, he told me he was doing a viticulture diploma over in Blenheim and came to Tahunanui at weekends to study and to see his children, who lived with his ex-wife in town.

Across the way from us was a battered green van. One morning, unobserved, I watched two policemen search the vehicle from bonnet to back bumper. They even took off the wheels. After half an hour they pulled a small brown packet from the vehicle's underbelly and then sat waiting in their car until the occupier returned. I'd never noticed her before. Dressed in tight-fitting jeans and a lacy top with swirls of blonde hair cascading past her shoulders, she looked innocently doll-like, young and pretty – somebody's cherished daughter. She was taken off in the police car and never returned. Eventually the van was towed away.

I t was also in Nelson that inside my head, a place I was spending more and more of my time, I began to lose my grip. It seemed laughable in one's fifties to have an identity crisis, but I felt adrift, dislocated. At times I didn't know what I was doing away from home and everything I knew. I did a lot of brisk walking along the wide grey emptiness of Tahunanui Beach and gradually worked out what I thought was happening. I'd lost all my reference points. I was not the editor, the mother, the gardener, the dog feeder, the best friend, the horse whisperer – or anything really. Whatever I had put up as my identity had gone. I was just me, whatever that was. I felt naked and rather bleak.

After the loss of Rachel, I thought that any other loss would be paltry. It seemed impossible that anything, apart from the loss of one of my other children, could ever have much impact again. And I had therefore ignored the fact that all losses cause a level of grief. And the losses, even though they were voluntary, of my job, my friends, my home, my animals, my life as I knew it, had tipped me upside-down. I hoped I hadn't taken on sadness and a sense of detachment as permanent conditions.

This loneliness was not a matter of location or lack of company. It was a state of mind. The splendid environment of the beach – the curdled clouds of early morning over the distant mountains, the water sparkling like crushed ice, the ribbed stretches of sand dappled with wet light – did little to dispel my heavy mood. The natural world helped but could not, on its own, do the work of cleaning up my mind, of bringing my thoughts and perspectives into some sort of comprehensible order.

There was something else that haunted me. In the chaos that first followed Rachel's leaving, I had desperately tried to find some proof that life after death existed. Oh, to know there was a place where I could hold her and talk with her again. Apart from the comfort of it, there were things she and I needed to sort out. I read signs everywhere, clutched at any scrap of evidence, sought out people who had faith. But gradually I was forced to accept that for every notion in favour of an afterlife there was a contradictory notion, and that minds far more capable than mine could not come up with conclusive answers. I still hoped that some event, sign, apparition or higher knowledge would come along to convince me, but now that I had so much time to think I allowed myself to glimpse the terrible possibility that I might never see my daughter again. This did nothing to improve my state of mind.

It took a lot of hard self-talking to stop those feelings of unarticulated dread and to convince myself that, since no amount of tears, flowers, prayers or research would ever fill the yawning hole that Rachel left behind, I was charged with turning aside from the chasm. And that meant ceasing my whimpering and adjusting to the current changes.

Keeping Going

O nce I'd made up my mind to live to the best of my ability, events contrived to reinforce my decision. There was nothing whimpering about the Gypsy Fair that came to town, bringing with it a flamboyant style of life on the road and public displays of dancing, tinkering, feasting and fortune hunting. This New Zealand band of gypsies had begun roving nine years earlier. There were only six house trucks then, but now there were over fifty and they called their village Atchintan, the old Romany word for parking place. In the winter they dispersed until the weather warmed up again and they began the next circuit of the country.

Many of the mobile dwellings were masterpieces of Kiwi craftsmanship, packed with character as well as the owner's worldly goods. Some were small and cosy, others palaces on wheels with televisions, freezers, computers, solar heating, wood burners, washing machines and dryers, and liberally decorated with curtains, photographs, artworks and ornaments and, on the balconies, herb and flower gardens.

During the week the citizens of Atchintan camped beside a river and made ready for the next fair. There were some decent artists among them making jewellery, woven garments and wooden bowls, and there was a good deal of entertainment such as a mouse circus, pony rides, belly dancers, jugglers, fire-dancers, performing dogs, tarot card readers and palmists. More interesting to me was how the gypsies had got to this point in their lives. They were not a bunch of itinerant ne'er-do-wells. A retired hospital matron, school teachers, a physiotherapist, an industrial chemist, a paramedic, a mechanic and a former police drug squad officer had all been part of their ranks. They said that unlike their European counterparts they rarely ran into any prejudice or resentment.

A woman, dressed the part in a long pink skirt and matching headscarf, her ankles, fingers, ears and toes festooned with silver jewellery, was dancing. She laughed at the delight of it, her skirt swirling, arms aloft, jewellery rattling like a burglar's bag. When she stopped to rest and flopped down on the steps of an old painted caravan I sidled over to introduce myself.

Jill Romain, who with her husband Rob was one of the driving forces behind the fair, had been on the road for twenty-nine years. I asked her if she'd have time for me to come back and talk with her when the fair was over.

'Of course,' she said. 'About ten in the morning would suit me. We'll be here packing up.'

Next morning I found myself in a comfortable lounge chair in her enormous house bus built inside an articulated Mercedes truck. It had all the comforts of home – washing machine, copper sink, wooden bench, oven, pot-belly stove, television and sound system, separate bedrooms, bookshelves and a fully equipped office and stairs that led to a pop-up lounge room on the second storey.

Jill heated water on the gas ring and made two mugs of herbal tea. We sipped it as she entertained me with a potted version of how all this became her life.

'Even as a child in England I was a rover, because of my father's work,' she said. 'I married Rob while we were still students and we probably would have settled down to a pretty unremarkable middle-class existence if it hadn't been for one small event that changed everything.

'I was sitting at the kitchen table flicking though a newspaper and I saw this small advert: "Wanted. A reliable mechanic for the Ford dealership, Accra, Ghana."

'"Where on earth's Ghana?" Rob said. A month later we were flying off to West Africa for two years. We had a great time and my first child was born there. But then a coup ended it all. We were given money and told to leave by whatever means we could.'

They decided to turn disaster into opportunity by crossing the Sahara by Land Rover on the way back to England. Three other adults came with them.

'I think that journey was a blueprint for the rest of our lives. It was really tough but fascinating. There were heaps of challenges to overcome but I can remember trying to slow down those last few weeks so we wouldn't have to return to normality.'

Normality no longer meant a semi-detached in the middle of industrial England. They bought a small island in the Orkneys and bred Viking North Ronaldsay sheep. And they bought their first bus.

'The island sheep eat seaweed,' she said, 'and so we went off bussing in the winter when there was plenty of it.'

Their family expanded: another daughter was born, they adopted a Thai-American boy who'd been abandoned after the Vietnam War, two Pakistani-English brothers whose mother was unable to look after them, a ten-year-old boy from a children's home in London, and a part-Nigerian, part-Polish twelve-year-old who'd also spent many years in a children's home.

'Off we'd go, all nine of us in the bus, for months at a time,' Jill said with a grin at my astonishment.

'How on earth did you all fit in?'

'Oh it was fine. We all had beds, I mean it was pretty comfortable. I was a teacher and I home-schooled the children and we travelled further and further afield until, in 1987, we just seemed to keep going east.'

They travelled through Europe, Turkey, Iraq, Saudi Arabia and the United Arab Emirates, and in Dubai put the bus on an Arab dhow bound for Karachi. For three years they wandered Pakistan, India and Nepal.

'I never felt I wanted to go home,' Jill said. 'We sold the farm while we were in India and, since then, the bus has been the only home I know. We're at home wherever we go.'

I nodded as if we were in the same league, which of course we weren't.

From India it was to Asia and Bangkok for some of the children to sit their 'A' and 'O' level exams at the British Embassy. After a few months the family sailed for Australia because Jill and Rob thought it was time to settle some of the children into jobs or university. Then they came to New Zealand and started the Gypsy Fair.

'Do you want to keep going?' I asked. 'Aren't you getting a bit tired of moving all the time?'

'If a real reason came up for us to stand still we would look at it,' Jill said, 'but at the moment putting down roots is out of the question.'

At eight o'clock the next morning I drove back to Atchintan to wish the villagers a happy journey. There was not a soul in sight. Apart from a few patches of crushed grass and wheel marks in the mud under the gateway it was as if they'd never been there.

I also became curious about an elderly woman who had spent much of her life on the road and was still driving about the country with her caravan. I'd seen a small piece about her in the *Nelson Mail*.

It was an easy matter to find her phone number and I rang her at nine o'clock one morning. 'Would you mind if I came and talked to you about your caravanning?' I said. 'I read that you are still dashing about the country.'

She giggled girlishly. 'Oh, I wouldn't say dashing. I don't think there's anything special about it. I've been caravanning all my life.'

Dorothy was a small, sprightly woman. Framing a lively face was a frizz of white hair and she wore an air of well-nourished good humour. I found it hard to believe her when she told me she was eighty-five.

'Now then, let me tell you,' she said, getting down to business. 'In 1929 my father, Ernie Chamley, built what I think was the first caravan in New Zealand. He was a cabinetmaker. Come inside and I'll show you the photographs.'

On the table in the kitchen she had spread out small prints that depicted in blurry sepia a small box-shaped affair that opened out each side. 'The top became the sides and the sides became the base,' she said. 'Then a canvas sheet pulled over a ridge pole became the roof. My father made that on my mother's sewing machine.'

I tried to make out what attached the caravan to the Tin Lizzie that pulled it. 'Oh, there was no tow bar on the car,' said Dorothy. 'We just had this thick rope that pulled it along. Of course you couldn't back it. If you wanted to turn it around you had to untie it, turn it manually and then tie it up again. It was a prototype for the pop-top caravans that were later manufactured commercially, I think it was in Wanganui.'

When Dorothy married Alex Williams her husband built their first caravan, a sophisticated affair by comparison, made of tempered hardboard with an aluminium roof spotted with putty in the nail holes. It had a curved back that you could lift up like the boot of a car.

'Of course there was no shower or sink or anything as complicated as that,' Dorothy said. 'That was in 1954, and when we went away in it we would stop on the side of the road wherever we liked. Alex and I had a few caravans after that. In the fifty-eight years we were married we often toured around the South Island but we never toured the North Island because we were afraid of the traffic there. Alex said that if I was driving up there he'd get out and walk. I said if he was driving I wouldn't even get in the car.'

Alex had died four years before.

The day I met her, despite the looming wet weather, this intrepid octogenarian was too busy to talk for long. She was packing for a month's trip around the lower half of the South Island with the Nelson Caravan Club. Her current caravan was pulled by a 1975 V8 Holden Statesman de Ville with a vinyl top. Streamers fluttered gaily from the aerial. All up, the length of the car and the caravan was 13 metres. That was a fair length for a woman of diminutive height to manoeuvre, but Dorothy was not about to let that stop her. 'I have to get a man to get it out of the shed and I can't back it, but there's usually someone around to do it for me.'

In the front seat of the V8 an enormous white teddy bear was held up by the seat belt. It wore a large red floppy hat. On the back seat there was another bear of similar proportions.

'I take safety precautions,' Dorothy said, giving a little wriggle of satisfaction with the arrangement. 'Benjamin Bear and his wife in the back make it look as if there are other people in the car. I'm a bit vulnerable you know, being this old and on my own and in a car that a lot of young hoons would love to get their hands on. I also carry a personal alarm and a whistle. You can't be too careful can you? Not these days.'

A few days later I could have done with a whistle myself. I was in the habit every morning of walking up the steep bush incline that led to the top of Botanical Hill, which was commonly known as the centre of New Zealand. The actual geographic centre was somewhere out at sea but it was from Botanical Hill that the city of Nelson was originally surveyed.

That morning was one of the region's finest. The air was freshly stoked, the sun was sharp enough to throw a mosaic of shadows through the canopy of trees onto the path. As I climbed, the faint hum of the city floated up to me but here on the hill I was cocooned in the swirls of green and gold. I thought I was alone.

Then without sound or warning a small scrawny man with large overlapping teeth stepped out from behind a tree to stand on the path in front of me. Sunlight shone through the huge ears that stuck out from the side of his head and lit their tips so that they glowed bright pink and gave him the appearance of a large rat.

I jumped. There it was – the ancient nightmare – sinister man lurking in forest comes upon and ravishes maiden fair. Well, grey actually.

He gave me a rodent-like smile. 'Great tit,' he said.

My mind froze and contracted. Tit? Two tits?

'Whaaaat?' My voice sounded pitiful.

'Great 'n't it?' he repeated. 'The day…' He flapped a large hand towards the sky. 'Great!'

'Oh, the day. Yes, yes, great. Really great.'

I fled up the path and, despite a burning chest and an agonising ache in my calves, I didn't pause until I got to the top. I felt undone and rather foolish.

My brush with Ratty didn't put me off my daily climb. From the summit, at 147 metres above sea level, there was a marvellous view of Port Nelson, Tasman Bay and the city with all its colourful houses spilling over the slopes and ridges of the hills. I used to half close my eyes and try to imagine, without much success, what it might have been like here in 1867. That was the year that my great-grandparents arrived from England aboard the *Cissy*.

My great-grandfather was the Reverend Bach Wright Harvey and he was married to Anne Sophia. They had made the journey with their two children, one of whom was my grandfather, and with Bishop Suter and his wife. They lived in Nelson while they awaited the Bishop's decision as to where my Reverend great-grandfather would be best to set up a new parish. This turned out to be in the raw, remote gold-rush town of Westport.

Anne had written many letters to her mother about the voyage and her time in Nelson and somebody (probably her mother) copied them into a small leather-cornered book that, over a century later, found its way into my own mother's care and then mine.

Standing on the hill 135 years after Bach and Anne Harvey had landed, I watched a massive modern ship manoeuvre past Haulashore Island and through the Cut to berth with weighty delicacy at Port Nelson. I forced my imagination to bridge the gap – to conjure up the image of the *Cissy* sliding towards land and the excitement there must have been on board after so many hard months at sea.

As she packed her boxes ready for disembarking in this strange land on the other side of the world, Anne wrote of her feelings:

Looking over the nice clean linen etc and all your many works and presents, is very dreary work and makes me very homesick. I do wish there was some way of expressing in writing what one feels – but it is very difficult. When I look over this letter it seems so cold and stupid – yet no words could express how thankful we should be to see any one of your dear faces, after all these strange people. I feel as if it were a just punishment for me for never having valued you enough but I shall try and not merit it now and we shall all meet bye and bye, my dear dear darling Mother. I love you now and always quite as much as in the days when I cried myself to sleep because I could not say good night to you – now I hug you inwardly and am satisfied, or try to be so. It seems as though all my friends were dead and almost as if I were dead with them – but that cannot be true because I am getting quite fat.

Anne never saw her mother again.

There was something similar, I thought, about our feelings of dislocation, but her isolation was so much greater than mine. I could email, text or phone my friends and family whenever I felt the need. Anne's letters might take three or four months to get to her family and friends and the same amount of time to receive a reply; and she faced the very real possibility that she would never go home. She wrote to her mother:

> I need scarcely say how we prize your letters. They are like daily (or monthly) bread. I do not know how we could struggle on without them. I must own to feeling it a great relief to find no great piece of news. I always dread for anything to happen.

Anne's new lifestyle was more changed than my own. I'd swapped a comfortable house in the suburbs of Auckland for the Tahuna caravan park. She'd come from the security of the refined parlours of well-to-do England to a place at the other end of the world that was only just feeling its way into some sort of order.

She wrote of the lack of home help:

> Mrs. J Richmond has children without number and actually managed at first without a servant, scrubbing her own floors. Still she is a thorough lady and looks like one and I look upon her (and upon all real ladies who have gone through such drudgery) as a sort of heroine. I really do feel glad not to have led this sort of life from the first, or I should have grown up a mere general servant. I am sure – now it does me good.

The Nelson she knew and the one I now explored were two vastly different places. I found a photograph of the town taken in 1864, when the population was about 7000 not its present 52,000. The hills were treeless and unmarked by any man-made structure. The few handfuls of buildings were scattered across the valley floor like doll's houses. The only one of any size was the wooden church on the hill, where Anne and Bach would soon worship on Sundays.

It was Anne's admiration for ladylike behaviour and her determination to entertain in style despite the privations of the colony that prompted me to throw a dinner party for four in the caravan. I invited Bill's brother Graham and his wife Pam by way of a gold-embossed invitation card with a request for RSVP and formal dress. They turned up in a tuk-tuk, he in a dinner suit and she in a long gown, fur cape, pearl earrings and matching necklace.

I'm afraid that there the pretence of refinement ceased. We drank too much, argued raucously, and next morning the interior of the caravan looked as if an elephant's stomach had exploded. I was not sure that in the 1860s such abandoned levity would have been the hallmark of a successful social occasion.

After two months Bill and I were so familiar with Nelson, and so enamoured of the place, that we were in danger of becoming permies like Joanna and Marion. Had it not been for Garry, who wanted a house painted at Ligar in Golden Bay, we might be there still.

Blue Moon Rave

A long the mudflats of the Kina estuary there was a tradition of writing in the sludge with large stones. At high tide they were covered with water but low tide revealed their glistening messages. 'It's a boy.' 'Doing our thing, yahoo.' Most of them were love messages or egotistical statements that mean little to anyone else. 'Barry loves Averil.' 'Karl and Sheree were here.' One, however, proved prophetic. 'High on life.' I had to slow down and crane my neck to read it.

Not far past the estuary, on the other side of Motueka, the road snaked up the Takaka Hill to 760 metres, from where we looked across the broad Takaka and Cobb valleys, the high wilderness beyond and the great scoop out of the north-western corner of the South Island called Golden Bay. From the top of the hill I felt like flying from the peak I was on to a ridge I could see on the other side of the valley. It was a high, sunshiny day, as bright as polished silver.

But it wasn't the sunshine that earned Golden Bay its name. It was first called Murderers Bay, then Blind Bay, Massacre Bay and Coal Bay but in 1857, when pig hunters found some gold nuggets up behind the present-day Collingwood, it finally received the name that has stuck for 145 years. It could just have easily been named Golden Bay for the little coves and tidal beaches that lined its curving shore and were covered in coarse orange-coloured sand.

We camped at Tata Beach, on the south-eastern shore of the bay. The section close to the water's edge belonged to a friend in Nelson. 'Stay as long as you like,' she had said. 'There's nobody much there in winter.'

Now that the summer was over, the little community had, in fact, dwindled to about ten people. The only sounds that penetrated the silence were the melodious calling of tui and bellbirds from the trees on the cliff, and the sea turning page after endless page against the sand. We could see a smudge of land shimmering in the distance – Farewell Spit – and in between a great stretch of shallow sea that rippled like corrugated iron and picked up the colours of the sky.

It took us about thirty minutes to drive to Takaka and any form of urban life. I drove in there every second or third day to buy groceries and download my email through my mobile phone. The cellphone signal was weak, which forced me to drive around to find a spot where the signal came through. Then I jumped out of the driver's seat, set up the hardware in the back of the truck and hoped the signal didn't fade in the meantime.

This contact with home and the outside world was a matter of some excitement. I seldom made phone calls because of the cost. Our snail mail, which was sent to the local poste restante, only arrived about once a month. So email was my best form of contact. How things had changed. Back at *Pacific Wave* my relationship with this technology had been strained. My inbox overflowed with things that had to be dealt with. Now I was often disappointed with its thin content.

Takaka was a one-street town with a tiny theatre, a butcher's shop, a collection of craft and junk shops, a museum and art gallery, a supermarket, a few cafés and two hotels. It served the 6000 inhabitants of Golden Bay well enough that their trips 'over the hill' didn't have to be too frequent. The place had always attracted people interested in some sort of radical change, either in their own lives or in society. They were not seekers of revolution but of self help and expanded possibilities, and refugees from the materialistic and consumerist culture of the mainstream. I came across a man called Ray who had arrived recently from a rural part of the Waikato. He called such people the 'oooom, golden glow types'. And he looked to the sky and made a moon circle with his arms to embellish the description. For him it was a big culture shock to find there were people like that in the world.

Down the footpath came a tall figure in a sweeping coat of purple and pink. He had a long, grey Father Time beard and his dark hair was tied in a knot at the back of his head. He viewed the world quite literally through round rose-tinted spectacles and he glided along in a lordly manner as if the fortunes of Takaka balanced on the tip of his nose.

On the other side of the road a gaggle of youths lounged on benches in the sun. Their get-up was, to say the least, expressive. One had an astonishing hairstyle that looked as if a deeply cyanosed hedgehog had perched on his head. His mate, a boy of about seventeen, had a jeweller's shop of silver rings protruding from his eyebrows, ears, lips, nose, tongue and neck. If he had undertaken this mutilation to gain attention it certainly worked on me.

Outside the chemist's shop stood a man with long, undisciplined hair that was weather-bleached at the ends. He wore a feathery decoration around his neck and a worse-for-wear Akubra jammed on his head. None of his teeth were in evidence. He had taken off his gumboots and placed them neatly together to one side, revealing knobbly feet clad in tattered and unmatched socks – one black and one bright pink. He was attempting to amuse a group of three young boys by doing sad little tricks with a ball and a piece of string. The boys were not impressed.

'Get a proper job,' they yelled derisively.

78

'I don't want to work,' said the juggler. 'If I work I have to pay taxes.'

'Yeah, well, why should we give you money that we've earned and paid tax on then?'

'Giving is good,' said the man with cheerful and implacable righteousness.

I almost gave him fifty cents for the entertainment.

These maverick souls mixed happily with earnest students of alternative lifestyles and a smattering of greybeards. They gravitated to the workshops and explored such meditative happenings as the First Sphere Weekend of the Ishaya Ascension for full human consciousness, the Blue Moon Rave, Crystal Channelling and Rune Readings, the Awakening of Genetic Memories while Stomping with Friends, and Tuning In to the Great Mother on an organic hazelnut farm.

I repaired for coffee to the Wholemeal Café, where I shared my table with a woman whose face had a cast of plump self-indulgence. 'Well, did you ever?' she said, indicating with sniggering scepticism the ball-and-string man, who was now standing at the café counter spending the miserable earnings of his street theatre.

'He shouldn't be allowed in here,' she whispered conspiratorially.

I said nothing. I'd always enjoyed the independence of misfits, dropouts and dreamers, and admired their indifference to what others regarded as the norm. Being brought up with the mores of respectability and godliness had, of course, made me ache for the other side of the tracks. In Hawke's Bay being middle-class meant golf or rugby on Saturdays and church on Sundays. Middle-class fathers drank at the club not the pub and they wore slouch hats and tweed jackets or gaberdine raincoats. Middle-class mothers wore twin sets, straight skirts well below the knee and sensible shoes. It was considered 'common' to sweat or swear, or to have tattoos or pierced ears.

I had yearned to be a Widgie – to wear tight black leather and lean against the pillion of my Bodgie's motorbike outside a milkbar, looking wizard as I pouted my green lips. But I was too timid to go off the rails. I went instead to chaperoned school dances and wore a polka-dot skirt puffed up with petticoats and tied at the waist with a pink cummerbund.

In Golden Bay thirty years later, I thought I might call myself Esther Delicious and buy a tie-dyed skirt.

Each day Bill went off with his paint pots down the road to Ligar Bay. Sometimes I walked over there – past the lagoon where an old sailing boat lay rotting in the dark, still water, past the spit of land where a few scruffy fishermen's cottages leant into the sand – to take him lunch. I dawdled on the way to watch the clouds scud across the sky or the wind lazily puffing through the long grass and gannets plunging for their own lunch out at sea.

At other times I walked along the orange sand of Tata Beach and picked up shells and stones and put them down again. Some days, to say that nothing happened was a wild overstatement. But I was learning the value of the state of nothingness. It was a great, light space where I could float in any direction – the antithesis of my old frantic life with its claustrophobic weight of deadlines and responsibilities.

One evening while I was sitting on a log by the sea as the sun went down it came to me that, Rachel aside, all the losses I lamented also spelt freedom. I was on the road, where nobody knew anything more about me than what I wanted to tell them, and for the first time in thirty years I was my own person. I laughed out loud at nothing and the laughter turned to a yell. And there I was, alone on the darkening beach howling at the rising moon. There would be other cares and other times, but I had, for this moment, the kind of unfettered joy I never thought I'd feel again.

. . .

In my diary, which was otherwise rather empty, I had boldly ringed the 10th of June in red. It was to remind me that I had a deadline that day for a lucrative project I was doing for a publisher in Auckland. Naturally it was not quite finished, so I had marked the day down for duty.

But it was such a glassy morning, the sea like light blue tissue paper, the leaves on the trees soft and shiny. I'd missed too many times like this because of an overblown sense of responsibility. So I tucked my conscience out of sight in my armpit, packed a little picnic, and drove the twisted miles to Totaranui Bay for a walk through the bush.

Heavy dew hung on the low bushes before I entered the deeper forest and it highlighted magnificent little orb webs that sparkled like diamond necklaces. I glimpsed a fernbird flicking around the marsh reeds. They were shy, diminutive birds rarely seen for any length of time, but just to know they were there was satisfying. The tide was out and as I started to climb I looked back at the golden sand of the inlet swathed across the valley like swinging hair and disappearing into a rigid sea of reeds. I could see D'Urville Island across the top of Tasman Bay quite clearly.

I tramped Pukatea Walk for about 40 minutes looking for the track to Anapai Beach but, my ability to find my way around in the bush being what it is, was back where I started before I realised I was on the wrong track. I began again and this time the path led me up a bluff, down a beautiful valley of mature trees and frothy ferns and along a ridge of tall kanuka, before dropping down to a wide, ginger-sanded beach. The bay, bounded by huge bluffs at one end, was not merely empty, there was nothing to indicate that anyone had been there in weeks.

Two little fishing boats, just specks on the wide horizon, were the only signs that I was not alone on the planet. I put my back against a log by the sea and ate my lunch. The peace was like a warm blanket, the only sounds the intermittent rustle of my plastic lunch bag and the waves sighing against the sand.

On the way back I was briefly joined by a young man humping a large pack. He wore only heavy boots with thick socks, a pair of ragged shorts and a navy bush singlet. With him were two business-like brindled dogs. Gavin was a pig hunter and was returning from three days al fresco. He didn't get a pig, he told me, and he'd lost his dog Thud. He left his bush singlet on the grass at the edge of the bush.

'Thud'll come out eventually,' he said. 'I'll leave this and she'll smell it and know to wait for me here. Stupid getting lost like that. She gets a bit carried away in there I reckon. I'll come back in tomorrow and pick her up. She's got a bloody mind of her own I tell you.'

'Why do you call her Thud?'

'At home she sleeps on the bed with me and that's the noise she makes when she jumps down and lands on the floor in the morning. She's a big dog.'

I worried about Thud and before I drove out of the bay about an hour later, I went back to where Gavin had left his clothing. There was Thud, a big black dog of indeterminate breeding, curled up on the singlet looking extremely comfortable and unconcerned. She didn't even bother to look up as I drove past.

Asbestos Cottage

We were smitten by Golden Bay's marvellous entanglement of forests, beaches, mountains and estuaries. We rode horses up Old Man Rock, kayaked along the sea coves of Abel Tasman National Park, took a bus to the tip of Farewell Spit, walked across the hills and on some of the bush tracks that led into the hinterland, drove around the Whanganui Inlet to the Anatori River – and still felt we had hardly begun to see it all.

The eastern part of the bay lay between the great wilderness areas of Kahurangi National Park at one end and Abel Tasman National Park at the other. On the west coast there were wild sculptured beaches and rocky promontories, and between the two areas mudflats and mangroves, forest and farmland, and the purest water in the world at Waikoropupu Springs. Someone told me you could lie on the bottom of the lake and still see the stars through the water.

Twenty minutes' walk over hilly farmland at the end of the Puponga Road brought us to Wharariki Beach on the western coast. It would be hard to find a more extravagantly dramatic bit of coast anywhere. Every time we were there its mood had altered and its great hills of soft-grey sand, moulded by the wind into ribbed peaks and gullies, were continuously shifting and reforming. Sinking into the sand on a hot day was torture; to struggle over it in a wind was to be sand-blasted with stinging grit that we then carried home with us in every crease and crevice.

Out beyond the dunes the swollen ocean hissed with menace as it ran in over vast areas of flat sand and left it glistening in the slanted light. It bashed against the gigantic rocky islands that wallowed offshore like beached whales, and clawed its way into the great caves that have been gouged from the cliff faces. A heavy spray often hung in the air, draping the scene in grey gauze and adding to the chilly isolation. On one such day the only other creature on the beach was a black-backed seagull. It stood defiantly facing the wind at the edge of the sea, swivelling every time a gust snatched at its feathers.

Explorations inland led us to the discovery of one of the country's most romantic pioneering stories. One bright cool Sunday in June we drove the Safari up the Cobb River valley into the craggy ranges high above sea level that form part of Kahurangi National Park. Then we walked for over an hour along a rocky track up through the podocarps and beech trees, which, even though we only carried day packs, was quite hard going for a couple of city slickers. We stopped on the lip of an abandoned asbestos mine to eat our lunch. My legs felt ataxic.

'Do you think we could turn back after this?' I begged. 'I'm bushed after that climb.'

'There's a hut a bit further up that I'd like to have a look at,' Bill said. 'And anyway it'll do you good to stagger on a bit after that chocolate you've just eaten.'

The hut was another hour-and-a-half further on up a much rougher and steeper path, but as it turned out I'd have walked twice as far to find, in a small clearing, the small, spartan, two-roomed bush hut known as Asbestos Cottage. It was a simple affair, but in the room that once served as living room and kitchen (so small you could hardly swing a possum in it) a mysterious story began to unfold. On one wall hung the blurry photograph of a man and a woman. She was tall, full busted, upright and dressed in a spotted Edwardian dress with a cap on her head and a ruff of fur around her neck. Her jawline was too strong for beauty and her eyes kept their distance. She stood next to a smaller, scrawny man, who wore a brimmed hat and was standing with his arms folded in a way that asserted some authority.

But it was the caption that really caught my attention. It named them – Annie and Henry Chaffey – and then stated that they had lived in the cottage for thirty-eight years.

Outside there was an area around the hut that was cleared. 'I think this was a garden,' Bill said, pointing to a puny rose that still struggled for existence among the alpine grasses. 'And look, here's an old apple tree. It's pretty rotten.'

We poked around a bit longer and photographed the hut inside and out, then headed back down the track to civilisation.

Back in Takaka I spent the next week in the library piecing together the mystery of two incredible lives. The rose turned out to be a fragile memorial to Annie Selina Chaffey, who had planted roses there some fifty years earlier, and who for nearly four decades struggled to survive on that spot, in the belly of the bush among the bullying winds and clotted snow.

I couldn't imagine that she ever intended to spend more than half her life hidden from the world in a hut of pit-sawn timber way up in those rude mountains. She was educated at Timaru School and taught the arts of proper manners and perfect hostessing as required in the parlours of middle-class New Zealand society at the turn of the century. She married a local man and probably wished she hadn't. He was reported to be vicious, mean with money and often absent. In time they had two sons.

I couldn't find any reference to how in the middle of this misery she met Henry Chaffey, a local miller who was escaping his own disastrous marriage, nor any whisper of their growing affection. In

1908 Timaru society, far from keeping records of it, would most likely have shuddered at such a liaison. But there was a report of how in 1913 Annie deserted her husband and sons and followed Henry Chaffey to the hide-out that he had prepared for her in the remote, bush-mantled mountains high above the Cobb River. She was thirty-four years old; Henry was forty-three. Annie never saw her parents, her husband or one of her sons again.

She could only have been obsessively infatuated with Henry or bruised beyond endurance to be able to do such a thing. Apparently it wasn't society's reprisals that the couple feared, but those of Annie's husband should he ever find them. As added security Henry called himself Charlie Fenton for a time.

The place was extremely remote, 900 metres above sea level and an arduous two-day walk from the first smudge of civilisation. There were no comforting neighbours, no telephone nor any other means of communication. Annie did not set eyes on another woman for the next seven years. To live in such raw exile would have been as tough a test of love as you could find, but it was obvious that Annie was no shrinking violet. She'd come to carve out a new life and that was what she did.

Henry cleared the bush, dug a garden and continued his prospecting and hunting for deer and goats. Once a fortnight he walked out for supplies. He left the hut at two in the morning and completed the 56-kilometre return trip at four the following morning. The loads this wiry little man carried on his back were legendary. He could lug a 55-kilogram pack uphill, pausing only to swig from the bottle of whisky he made sure was handy. A full bottle at the start of the trip was often empty at the end of it.

Much of what the couple ate was the result of their own labour, although nurturing plants to edible maturity must have required determination. The garden was vulnerable to almost anything the elements could throw at it. But Annie was a planter who put down roots in more ways than one. The only time she left the cottage while she lived there was on a stretcher on her way to Nelson Hospital when she had colitis, supposedly from eating weka meat that was not properly cooked.

Just existing was a full-time task. Annie made cheese from their goats' milk and she made soap from fat, caustic soda and wood ash. She made all her own clothes, dressing in the long skirts and high collars of Edwardian fashion. She smoked and was partial to much more than a medicinal tot of brandy, both of them distinctly unorthodox habits for a woman at the time. She wrote copious letters and occasionally sent family and friends presents such as native snail shells, weka oil for rheumatism, jams and pickles, and once the beak and feet of a kiwi.

I could feel the ache of Annie's loneliness. The man she'd made the centre of her life was often away over the hills, sometimes gone for ten days at a time. He was gone when the stags were roaring and bashed their terrifying antlers against the hut, and away in 1921 when the Murchison earthquake tore chunks from the flanks of the mountains and hurled them down the valley. He was often absent when the wind threatened to rip the roof from their puny shelter and snow hissed against the windows.

Henry's prospecting turned up small finds of gold, but his faith for the future lay more in asbestos. Annie sometimes helped him bring loads of serpentine rock back to the hut and at night by the fire they broke out the threads of high quality fibre, which Henry carried out of the bush on his back. Asbestosis had never been heard of.

Henry, in trying to get mining companies interested in working the deposits around their hill, came to the notice of Mr Hume, an Australian interested in both the asbestos deposit and the potential development of a hydro station in the area, and who saw the economies of building one road to do both jobs. And so a dam and hydro station were planned on the Cobb River and a road was begun in 1937.

Civilisation was creeping closer to Asbestos Cottage. Henry was employed as a caretaker on the asbestos mine and no longer had to go to Motueka for supplies but to Takaka by an extension of the route Bill and I had climbed. Annie was unimpressed with modern developments, except for the addition to her life of a radio, which released her from her haunting solitude.

There were also more visitors. The story went that if Annie chose to entertain she was as attentive to niceties as any suburban hostess. And because she insisted on dressing for guests there was often a notice at the beginning of the track that led to the hut that read 'Shout from here and wait' or 'Cooee or fire a shot for Chaffey' and sometimes 'No callers for Mrs Chaffey as she is making raspberry jam'.

There'd been no cooee when we had arrived at Asbestos Cottage, just a stinging silence. The fire grate was empty and, except for the rose and a clump of cosmos, there were no flowers in Annie's garden. Along the track we'd noticed chips from the rock made by a prospector's hammer, the only sign that Henry had ever passed that way. There was no marker to indicate where he fell and died in the snow on his last journey in 1951, just short of home. He was eighty-three years of age.

At the door of the cottage I had placed my feet on two worn stones and squinted into focus some tiny vehicles snaking their way up the distant Takaka Hill. These were Annie's only visual links with a world outside her own. I would have liked to have slipped in beside her, to give her a hand with the jam making or roasting the weka, and to ask her if she regretted coming to this place or if she resented Henry for his drinking and his long absences. And did she still love him after all that togetherness.

I guessed that she did. When he was found dead she returned to their cottage, shut herself in, doused everything in kerosene and set it alight. But either the damp or divine intervention halted the flames. The smoke brought rescuers from the asbestos mine and she was taken down to Takaka and later to relatives in Timaru.

In her absence cars had arrived in the town as well as electricity, telephones, fridges and washing machines. The noise was unbearable and the lifestyle a mystery. She spent a lot of time in her room with cigarettes and a bottle of brandy.

Two years was enough. In 1953 she withdrew her small savings from the bank, rolled them up in a note to her eldest son and threw the bundle over the neighbour's fence. She burnt all her clothing in the grate of the fire in her room, dressed herself in her best nightgown, swallowed all her sleeping tablets and lay down on the bed.

Back in her hills I'd fetched water from the stream as she must have done a thousand times and in a sentimental gesture I'd soaked the rose and torn away the grass that threatened to smother it. The hut where Annie made jam and Henry wrote letters now had a historic rating that kept it repaired. But in the garden there would soon be nothing but grass. No one would clear it because the place belonged to the Chaffeys and the Chaffeys were gone.

Too Toffy for Takaka

Caravan life in Golden Bay proceeded quietly enough until the stir I unwittingly caused the day I put two slices of Vogel's in the toaster for a mid-morning snack. We were staying at the camping ground at Pohara Beach and I sat outside in the sun waiting for the signal that the bread had toasted to perfection, thinking life was good. I closed my eyes. My mind wandered.

The next thing a fellow camper, an ample woman clad in a light blue fluffy dressing gown, burst through the bushes like an outsize puffball screeching, 'Fire! Fire! Oh thank God you're all right. Don't panic. The brigade's on its way.'

I opened one eye and the word 'loony' entered my mind. Then, out of the corner of that same eye, I caught a glimpse of our home and castle lazily expelling from every orifice curling billows of smoke. To my rescuer's increased alarm, my response was to dash into the eye of the fire. I emerged holding aloft two wizened, glowing embers from the toaster that forgot to pop. We laughed so hard we almost omitted to phone the fire brigade to tell them to abort the mission.

I couldn't get rid of the smell of burnt toast for weeks.

With toast on my mind it was hardly surprising that, a few days later, I was stopped in my tracks when I saw, in the window of Takaka Gold & Silver in the main street of town, a wooden carving of a piece of toast popping out of a fish with a zipper along its back. It bore the signature of Theodore Arnold Gustafson, which was commonly written as TAG.

Further investigation inside the shop revealed more intricately executed wood-carvings by the same extraordinarily talented man. The *pièce de résistance* was a life-size dresser, which sagged and twisted as if it was in the process of an elegant faint. All its drawers were open and stuffed with detailed carvings of both likely and unlikely objects.

TAG had a thing about toasters. The everyday household appliance was carved surfing, sprouting antlers and acting punk. Toast sprang out of other unlikely objects apart from the fish and a piece flew across the screen on a carved television set with the caption *Toast in Space*. I was so taken with the zany humour of all this that I determined to find the man behind it. It wasn't hard to locate anyone in a place the size of Golden Bay, and when I phoned him he asked me to come to his workshop in East Takaka, but could I please tell no one where he was. He valued his privacy.

The shed was set beside a grove of native trees well back from the road. A tall thin man with a solemn face topped by a black beret came onto the landing to greet me. His overalls were splattered with paint.

'Hello there,' he said, waving a paint brush in the air. 'I'm trying some bright colours on some teapots.' The accent was American.

In an isolated and primitive disused woolshed lent to him by a local farmer, and with not much more than a bandsaw, drill, chisels and gougers, Theo turned out his playful carvings from wood he collected from farms and beaches: everyday objects such as a vacuum cleaner, a plate of biscuits, an ironing board or a lampshade were turned, by tipsy surfaces or association with other unlikely objects, into what he called explicit nonsense. A life-size lawn mower had two large cups on the handles, on an ironing board an iron had just flattened a tap from which water dripped onto the floor, carved wallpaper featured fried eggs, flapping fish clogged the nozzle of a vacuum cleaner.

'You have a wonderfully oblique sense of the ridiculous,' I told him.

'It's kitsch,' he said. 'I don't think people judge my work in terms of being beautiful or awful. They're just fascinated.'

'And delighted and surprised,' I said. 'What's the thing about toasters?'

He threw me a small smile that lifted the corners of his mouth but never reached his eyes. 'You haven't seen the biggest of them. It's eight square metres and an enormous bit of toast pops up from a drawer. I called it *Firewood* so that people would know I'm not seriously obsessive about toast.

'I've seen it,' I said. 'At Jester House, I think.'

'Yes, yes, that's it.'

I told him about my latest encounter with toast and I doubled up at my own joke.

Theo looked at me wistfully. 'I wish I could laugh like that.'

It was ironic that a man who could turn out quirky, humorous objects that lightened the hearts of everyone who saw them should confess that his biggest battle was with chronic, deep depression.

'In a way my work is therapy,' he said. 'There is a meditative quality to working in this environment, but I don't know where this humour comes from. I am not an especially humorous person.'

We talked about depression and he explained with candour a fearful dread that came from nowhere and never seemed to leave him – not with the love of wife and children, counselling or medication.

'I live in a sort of hell I can't understand,' he said, 'and I can't seem to find a way out.'

I'd only once felt the frightful void he talked about. It was a short, sharp journey into a pit so appallingly black that the only thought I had was that I couldn't stay there. And then it came to me that I didn't have to. The thought of suicide gave me a choice, and understanding I had an option was like turning on a light. It was that light – the beam of choice – that helped me pull myself back to a safer reality. Remembering that experience gave me a glimpse of what Theo's far greater hell might have been like. I said nothing.

I could not know that this gentle, quietly spoken man who talked to me of his inner agony as much as of his art would not be able to carry the burden too much longer. A year or so later Theo would quietly take his own life among the native trees beside the shed. His choice pulled him in a different direction, but I'll always think of him going towards the light.

Entertainment Golden Bay style offered some gripping options. One Sunday we were faced with the serious question of whether to go to the pig weigh-in at the Telegraph Hotel, bowls and gin at one of the local schools, the Golden Valley Country Music Awards in the Pohara Hall or quiz night at the Mussel Inn. The music won the toss. We paid $10 and sat on benches facing the stage while various talents solemnly crooned and strummed to an audience of about seventy. Some items were worthy of the stage; others were, frankly, awful, but performed with such enthusiasm that they were at least endearing. We slunk out the door before the end and hastened to Takaka to catch the pig weigh-in.

Behind the pub two chiller trucks had opened up their doors to reveal their grisly cargo. We joined the crowd of about 200 people who had gathered in the yard to watch the booty being weighed and measured. I was impressed by the judges' unflinching way of confronting the task. They were as prosaic as hangmen.

There were twenty-one pigs that day. Seventy hunters, divided into thirty-five pairs, had been out in the hills for two days and the lucky ones had carried their quarries home on their backs. Reece and Johnny Harwood won the longest tusk competition and Steve Chamberlain and Shane Eggers won the Pig of the Bay and the $500 prize with their boar of 63.5 kilograms. The carcasses were then auctioned off to the highest bidders. We could've picked up a whole pig for around $40, skin, tusks, tail, intestines and all four trotters. But what to do with it then? You couldn't skin a pig in a caravan.

We played golf most weeks at the rolling links course at Pohara. On my way to the tee off on the first day I went there, I crossed paths with four women golfers. They gave me rigid little smiles that conveyed disapproval, bringing sharply to mind a time when I was seventeen. On the golf courses of Hawke's Bay I had often been the victim of those frost-nipped smiles from some of the women of my mother's generation, presumably because I had transgressed some unwritten rule of etiquette. As an adolescent they terrified me, those striding women with their bossy presence and their squinty eyes constantly scanning for something to censure. They put me off golf for years.

On another occasion at the Takaka course we played a foursome with new friends Bill and Catherine from Patons Rock. We met up outside the clubhouse. I wore my standard golfing gear – blue check shorts of the length considered proper, a matching top and peak and a rather smart pair of golf shoes that had cost me an arm and leg.

'Oh my gawd. You're too toffy for Takaka,' cried Catherine. 'That's why you got those looks. That gear is far too smart for us.'

It was while we were staying at Bill and Catherine's on the beach at Patons Rock that we came across the most stylish bit of peripatetic wheel estate we were to see in our first two years of travelling. A new Mitsubishi Fuso, about 13 metres long, its livery of gold and black gleaming with polished attention, was parked in the small reserve at the end of the beach. Its windows were dark and, judging nobody to be home, we circled the vehicle muttering exclamations of admiration and envy.

We were mildly surprised when a window suddenly opened and a cheerful Maori face appeared.

'Gidday,' said the man, who introduced himself as Ray.

'Do you want to have a look inside?'

The other person in the bus, a woman, didn't look quite as eager for the intrusion.

'This is Gloria,' said Ray. 'I'm running off with someone else's wife – ha, ha. Everybody does that, don't they?'

It took us a few minutes to tune into Ray's waggish sense of humour. Gloria, who was in fact his wife, lit a cigarette and gave us a watery smile. 'You can come back in the morning for a bus tour,' said Ray. 'It's not a good time now. I've got the spa pool turned on.' We were impressed.

The next morning the image of opulence and order blurred slightly when we found Ray and Gloria enjoying the sun and a cup of coffee while sitting on hay bales they had dragged from the bus's luggage compartment. Still, hay bales or not, this was a mobile palace, modern in every detail – from the parquet floor, double-door fridge and freezer, full-size stove and all mod cons in the kitchen, to the well-padded lounge with its state-of-the art sound system and television embedded in the wall, the extravagant bathroom and the double bedroom crowned by a crystal chandelier. The spa pool turned out to be a hoax.

Ray wore his pride in this glorious home away from home like a ship's captain. He insisted we examine every nut, bolt and fitting on a tour that lasted well over an hour, and then he sat us down for a formal speech of thanks.

'I am honoured that you have taken the time for a complete tour of the Capricorn,' he said. 'And I am grateful for the chance of our meeting.'

We assured him the treat was ours.

. . .

Another treat was to go to the Junction Hotel for the roast of the day – cost $9. The Junction had kept true to the style of pub I used to see all over the country in the sixties. The bar was large and smoky with an open fire at one end. The separate dining room was immaculate: heavy burgundy-coloured velvet drapes at the windows, a floral carpet in red and brown, vinyl chairs and tablecloths of lace or white linen. Artificial rosebuds in a vase adorned each table, along with Worcestershire sauce in silver holders, silver salt and peppers shakers and silver cutlery. The kitchen was behind a screen on which hung a large round mirror with scalloped edges. At the other end of the room was a rather faded picture of sailing ships on the high seas.

The choice of food on the menu was also iconic sixties: nothing lay on a bed of anything else. There was no scotch fillet char-grilled and lying on roasted field mushrooms elegantly stuffed with cracked pepper pâté and drizzled with ginger, berry and red wine jus; and there were no noisettes or chorizo sausages, red onions in carbonara sauce or feta gnocchi. They didn't mess with menus around here: 'Hawaiian ham, steak, plate of chicken, roast vegetables, peas, chopped spinach and gravy.'

Bill and I chose the chicken, with double gravy please, and we accompanied the feast with a bottle of Mateus Rosé because we were starting to suspect that we were low on funds. The wine was the only unpalatable part of the meal. The food was generous and cooked to perfection and the mains were followed by a choice of sticky date or bread and butter pudding, Pavlova and fruit salad, or chocolate sundae. Coffee and tea was 'Help yourself at no extra charge' from the urns that sat on a table at one end of the room.

Nola was our waitress. She was neatly dressed in a pink uniform and was polite, swift and efficient. She also happened to be the manager, receptionist and sometime barmaid. She told me later that she had worked in hotels for forty years and had spent fifteen at the Junction. Now 'they' wanted her to sit exams for which she paid a $120 fee, to prove that she was capable of running a pub. 'I'm not sure how I'm going to write it all down,' she said.

We had become partial to less-than-perfect eating houses where the character was not themed or forced, where even if the service was sometimes casual to the point of non-existence the lack of pretension was, frankly, a relief. The Mussel Inn on the road to Collingwood was a good example, although there was nothing wrong with the service. The small, rustic restaurant and bar with a big reputation was in an old tin shed extended by an addition of locally sawn macrocarpa. In this friendly, chaotic room, the tables had benches and the shelves were stuffed with books and magazines. There was a large open fireplace at one end of the room. The place was dotted with memorabilia – a greasy slouch hat, a dirty teddy bear, feathers, pinecones, driftwood, a Buzzy Bee.

The walls were hung with posters. 'There's a man's job to be done,' read one. 'The Collingwood to Karamea Road. Enlist today. Report Browns hut 9 am with shovel and barrow.' It was a send-up of the current debate about the nonsense or commonsense of cutting a road from Collingwood through the almost impossible terrain of Kahurangi National Park to the West Coast. Another notice was addressed to smokers: 'According to the rules, half of this building is supposed to be smoke free for the purpose of dining. We haven't quite worked out exactly which half that is yet, so in the meantime, we would ask if you could show your consideration and try to refrain from your unfortunate habit while people are dining. Don't forget there are excellent views of the garden to be had from the veranda.'

The inn produced its own beers, which were traditionally brewed and unfiltered. From the list that advertised the excellent properties of drinks such as White Heron Wheat Beer, Pale Whale Ale, Captain Cooker Manuka Beer, Freckled Frog Feijoa Cider and Monkey Puzzle Ale, I chose the pale Golden Goose Lager taken with a slice of lemon. Bill singled out a beer called Strong Ox, which was the colour of burnt toffee.

We ordered steak and salad. The portions were big enough to feed a miner come down from the hills. I ate three-quarters of mine and even Bill, who had a robust appetite, left a sizeable mouthful or two. At the bench adjacent to ours sat three men, all sporting shaggy beards and wearing coarse tartan shirts. I caught snatches of their conversation, which was about the economics of growing organic vegetables in the bay. At the other end of their table a man sat on his own. He was small and dressed in a faded blue T-shirt and greasy jeans and he had the sort of dark complexion that came with too much outdoor living and too little soap and water. Like a dog that expected to be kicked he kept casting suspicious glances around the room.

I was a little startled to see him suddenly get up and move confidently to where we were sitting. 'Good evening,' he said, in a confiding and deferential tone. 'My name is Ben. I have been watching you sitting here with those plates in front of you and I thought I'd come and take them away. The staff are hopeless here. They let people like you, who are obviously used to better service, sit with dirty plates in front of them for hours.'

'Oh,' was all I could say. Bill's eyebrows shot up but he remained speechless. We'd only just finished eating.

Ben swooped on our offending dishes and, balancing one on his left hand and the other on his left forearm, turned and made for the kitchen. As he went his right hand moved rapidly and repeatedly from plate to mouth. Not a morsel was left by the time he reached the kitchen door. It all happened so swiftly that we hadn't even had time to register astonishment before he was back on his perch hunched over the table. He never looked at us again. I thought it wasn't a bad lurk if one was forced to live by one's wits – original anyway and hardly a criminal act.

In fact, there didn't seem to be much serious crime at all in

Golden Bay. Police notices reported in the *GB Weekly* ranged from the theft of a toolbox to a series of nuisance calls and a suspicious scrub fire. But nothing to make my hair stand on end. The people of Golden Bay seemed to be particularly community minded. Under another heading in the paper I read, 'As the driver of a white Bluebird, I apologise to the owner of a large tan campervan for the damage to his bumper. An impetuous action while under stress can cause embarrassment and later, possible futile contrition.'

Waiting for Godwits

The biggest dilemma that Golden Bay residents had to address was what to do for a living. There was no one much to employ you if you didn't employ yourself and there was a two-year stand down on the dole. Necessity encouraged enterprise and Golden Bay had the highest number of self-employed people in the country. There were candle makers and begonia growers, a salami maker, bush-walking guides, llama trekkers, a lily grower, artists, possum hunters, flax weavers and eel keepers, and a cactus grower who hoped to make his fortune from making a local version of mescal.

But of all the off-beat pursuits, occupations and callings that gave Golden Bay its eccentric personality, the one that mystified me the most was the existence of a man who called himself the Swami Mukti. He was much quoted around the bay and seemed to have a faithful following, and so it wasn't hard to trace his whereabouts to a retreat perched like an eyrie way up on the high hills near Birds Clearing. My own suspicions were that he would be either a con or endearingly out to lunch.

I took the Safari and my courage one Sunday and made the journey to the tops, wheeling through several streams and then juddering along a rock-strewn road that twisted upwards to end about 700 metres above the coast on rough pastureland. I opened a farm gate on which a roughly carved sign said 'Anahata Retreat' and, feeling like a trespasser, trod unctuously up a path that led to a rudimentary wooden building. The swami and a retreater were washing clothes in a basin on the verandah. They managed to look surprised, curious and friendly all at once.

'I won't bother you,' I called out. 'I'm just popping in to say hello.' It seemed a bit of a stupid thing to say, considering I'd just done 40 minutes of determined driving to get there.

'Welcome, welcome,' said the swami with a light accent that probably came from the Indian sub-continent. 'Come inside. How did you find us? My goodness, very few people just drop in here.'

The Swami Mukti was not dressed in saffron robes but in quite ordinary track-suit trousers and an orange sweater. His face made a strong impression on me. He had probably seen forty some time earlier but his skin, which was copper brown, was soft and unlined. His hair was close-cut, greying and beginning to recede, and his top teeth protruded slightly. But his eyes were his most impressive feature. They were brown and luminous with extraordinary clarity.

Inside the small building that served as a community hall was a kitchen, a communal area with chairs and bookshelves, a television and a lot of wooden floor space. The swami introduced me to his young wife, whose head was wrapped in a purple scarf. She glided softly forward on bare feet and bestowed a beatific smile. Her name was Karma Karuna. Their four-year-old daughter, who bounded around the room like an exuberant puppy, was called Sundari. The retreater came from Germany and had been there for several weeks. At home, he told me, he was a baker by trade.

'Come,' said the swami. 'I'll show you around.'

Moving with a fluid gait that belied his age, he led me into the native forest to show me a tranquil rondavel built of rammed earth where his pupils learnt to meditate and exercise. 'It's a beautiful room,' he said, enthusiastically. 'Very comfortable and quiet. We built it ourselves with help from the village. Many people came to help. We have good support from the village.'

Another round earth building further down the slope was used for accommodation. It was furnished with a double bed and a few necessities but looked rather damp. Outside again, the Swami Mukti pointed to a pipe in the ground. 'Here we have a well,' he said. 'Several years ago a water diviner came here and he told us to dig twenty feet on this spot and we would find water. Everybody was very sceptical about this but I had faith in him. And so we dug and there, exactly where he said, we found pure water.'

With his family the swami lived in a simple oblong hut further down the slope behind an organic vegetable garden. Its floors were bare and the only form of heating was a wood-fired stove.

'It can get particularly cold up here in winter,' he said. 'Sometimes it can snow.'

I looked down to the hills falling to the edges of the bay and did not doubt him. Up there it felt closer to the clouds than the sea.

Back in the community building, the swami sat on the floor in the lotus position, and managed to look as relaxed in that extraordinary entanglement of limbs as he would have lying on a cushioned lounger. We sipped herbal tea and he told me he had spent sixteen years in India with his guru, Paramahamsa Satyananda, and now specialised in teaching therapeutic yoga and the deeper aspects of holistic yoga that he believed had been lost on their journey to the West.

I was already convinced he wasn't a fraud. Instead I found myself regarding a man who possessed the kind of serenity that distinguished the spiritually enlightened – a radiant assurance developed from a lifetime of discipline and meditative practices.

'I am very curious to know how you have come to be on the top of a hill in a place like Golden Bay in New Zealand.' I said.

He edged away from the enquiry. 'Well, you see, it just came to be. There is no particular reason.'

I didn't see, but I left it at that.

There was a moment of silence and then he said to me, 'Where are you going?' It was a simple question but as it came from a swami I looked for a deeper meaning. I couldn't, however, find a deeper answer.

'When I leave here? Just down the hill to Pohara,' I said, scrabbling around in my mind for something more profound.

He seemed not to hear me. 'Aaaah,' he sighed. 'A mystery.'

I looked at him and gave what I hoped was a mysterious smile.

'Your purpose is to find out who you are,' he said.

I copied his sigh. 'Aaaah. Thank you.' I swallowed the last of my tea and rose to take my leave.

'You must come and stay with us,' said the swami. 'Any time at all, except when we are full, of course.'

It could have been very pleasant, I thought, to float around for a few weeks up there in the mountains looking, with the guidance of these peaceful people, for divine or cosmic connection. But I had Bill, who always had his feet planted firmly on the ground, and even now was down at the bottom of the mountain waiting for his dinner.

As I rattled down the hill I pondered how I could begin to find out who I was. Was I a meaningless accident or part of a divine plan? I couldn't even take a guess at it. I could work out *how* I was in terms of how I was feeling but *who* I was, essentially, when stripped of my worldly references, was indeed a mystery. Tucked away in my mind was a poem that sometimes, like a mantra or a tune I couldn't stop humming, came to the surface. It was written centuries ago by Li Po, a Chinese man with a sense of humour.

Hard is the journey.
Hard is the journey.
So many turnings
And now where am I?

It started up like a metronome as I drove towards the sea. I'll begin with what I know, I thought. I'm a middle-aged, rather ordinary woman with no great distinguishing features or locatable depth who lives in a caravan. And that was as far as it went.

Like a gigantic painting the whole bay had come into view below me, stretching out to merge with the sky. In the distance I could just make out the shimmering line of Farewell Spit. And having failed to come up with anything exciting in the attempt to discover my self, I began to consider instead its more intriguing existence. The sandy arc that formed the north-west tip of the bay was New Zealand in the making. Each year it was widened by about 3 million cubic metres of glacial silt and stones, which were swept up the west coast by the sea and dropped along its northern edge.

For me the most alluring aspect of the spit was not the famous bus ride over its sand dunes to the lighthouse at its tip but the fact that, at its base, the swamps, marshes and tidal mudflats were the feeding place for thousands of birds. The first times we were there, in June, many of the ninety species that had been recorded there had flown, except for the black swans that looked like bobbing question marks as they swam in their hundreds just out from the shore. I was surprised they didn't get seasick.

But in March the following year it was high season. Godwits had gathered by the thousand, forming forests with their spindly legs. They were delicate birds, their tummies at that time plump, their beaks long, thin and pink at the base. Many of them were a handsome rusty colour, which, together with their speckled backs, made them very well camouflaged against the sand. At midday they were facing into the strong wind and many had tucked their heads under their wings trying to sleep, to gather strength no doubt for the incredible 11,000-kilometre journey to Alaska and eastern Siberia on which they were about to embark. They were disturbed by large gatherings of pied oystercatchers that preened noisily and made forays into the godwit groups, upsetting their repose. It was all right for them. They only had to go to the North Island for the winter and up into the Southern Alps to breed. Among the godwits were scattered groups of lesser knots, which were smaller squatter birds that also journeyed to eastern Siberia. I wondered how many of them would make it.

It was amazing that creatures with such fragile frames protected from the elements by a mere handful of feathers could make these colossal odysseys. It made our own wanderings look pitiful by comparison. But, like the godwits, we knew when our time to leave Golden Bay had come. We had fallen so in love with the place that we'd looked at real estate there – and then looked at reality. There was nothing to sustain a painter or a writer there and our dollar level was falling like a barometer reading before a storm.

Ironically, one of the things I didn't enjoy about being on the move was moving. Once I'd settled in somewhere I found I would have preferred to stay. But I didn't want to make a fuss about leaving either. Like the gypsies in Nelson, it was better to be here today and gone tomorrow without farewells or ceremony or lingering glances. It was one of the ways of the road.

The Bounteous Vine

The top of Takaka Hill was littered with karst rocks that formed bizarre shapes like petrified debris from a forgotten battlefield. Beneath the surface there was a deep cave system that included the deepest cave in New Zealand. The only underground activity I could contemplate, however, had to be well organised with a good guide and good lighting. I was keen to dip into the bowels of the earth but I didn't fancy floundering around in the dark.

Bill didn't fancy floundering around at all. He tried several lines of argument. 'It's just a cave,' he said. 'We'll do it next time,' he said. 'We'll be late,' and, 'I'm hungry,' and finally, 'Why would anyone want to see a cave and a few old moa bones?'

'Because it's there,' I said, getting out of the car. 'And because you really don't want to. And because every now and then I like to win out.'

And so we descended into the 350-metre long Ngarua Cave, which was commercially run for timid speleologists. It was full of fantastic stalactites, stalagmites, textured walls, grotesque formations and great cathedral caves and recessed pits that made the tips of my fingers tingle when I looked into them.

About half way along in a muddy pool by the side of the path a cache of well-preserved moa bones had been discovered not so long ago and instead of being whisked away to a museum they had been left more or less as they were found. There was an almost entire skeleton of a bush moa, complete with gizzard stones and trachea bones.

'Strange creatures, moa,' I whispered to Bill, who was peering myopically at the gizzard stones, 'mysterious and other-worldly. Maybe they're not really extinct and one day someone will come across one like Orbell did with the takahe.'

'I doubt it. But what, I wonder, made them extinct in the first place? They'd be a bit much for a rat to bring down and it's hard to imagine that Maori hunters killed them all.'

A few days later in the library at Blenheim I came across a less-than-lucid explanation written by Mark Twain. 'The natives used to ride [the moa],' he'd written. 'It could make 50 miles an hour, and keep it up for 400 miles and come out reasonably fresh. It was still in existence when the railway was introduced into New Zealand, still in existence and carrying the mails – The company exterminated the moa to get the mail [business].'

The author was in New Zealand in 1890 because he had gone bankrupt to the tune of $100,000 and had undertaken to pay his creditors back by way of a lecture tour Down Under. We would be going bankrupt, too, if we didn't get somewhere to find some work. A quick mental calculation as we came over the hill had revealed that we were, indeed, seriously short of dosh.

'We could pick something or prune something,' Bill said. 'There should be something on around here.'

At the foot of Takaka Hill was the small village of Riwaka, surrounded by fields of tall hop vines. Hop gardens were not found anywhere else in New Zealand apart from a few plants I had seen growing wild in the hedges around Upper Moutere. I had an image in my mind of hop string-tiers walking down the rows of vines on stilts and it struck me as a fun way to earn a living. So in the centre of Riwaka I called out to a little man in a pointed cap who looked like an animated garden gnome as he knelt close to his front fence weeding a bed of pansies.

'Excuse me, can you tell me who I could talk to around here about the hops?' I asked.

He got up off his knees and jabbed his finger in the air. 'You'd best see Tom in that big house there. He's king of the hops around here.'

Tom Inglis turned out to be the chairman of the Hop Marketing Board and had been a grower for thirty years. He was courteous about my impromptu visit but warned that he'd just got back from a hop conference in Europe and was feeling a bit ragged.

'Still, if anybody gets me started talking hops it's like giving a reformed drunk a bottle of wine,' he began. 'Here in New Zealand hop growing is a family affair and descendants of the German and English settlers who first brought hops to the valley still grow them. You just have to look at the names in the business – Eggers, Drogemuller, Bensemann and Heine. We're a bit different because my great-grandparents came from Scotland with their hops. I'm a fourth-generation grower and my son is the fifth.'

Hops were apparently picky about where they grew. So it was lucky that the settlers who brought them in ended up in the only spot in New Zealand where the plants seemed to thrive. The hops I'd seen in the hedgerows were offspring of earliest varieties, engagingly named Fuggles and Goldings.

It was the wrong time of year for work and apparently I was about two centuries out of date about the stilts. There was stringing in October, when hundreds of strings were tied from ground level to a horizontal supporting wire 4.5 metres overhead. We said we might come back then if we hadn't found better things to do, but without the stilts stringing looked about as exciting a way to earn a living as plucking moa feathers.

At that time, in July, there was not much agricultural work around anywhere except in the vineyards, where labour never seemed to cease. By mid-November there was cherry picking in

Central Otago followed by the harvests of peaches, apricots, nectarines and plums. Then pip-fruit started to ripen and the grape vintage began, and those provided work until about mid-April, when kiwifruit picking in the North Island started. But when that was done most agricultural areas became dormant, waiting for the warmer weather. Grapevines were the only salvation for itinerant workers, along with a little kiwifruit and berry pruning and later in the winter the back-breaking harvest of asparagus. In the absence of any more maintenance work presenting itself, the vineyards seemed like our best bet and Blenheim was the place to head for that.

On our first night in Blenheim we were bidden by winery friends to the opening of an exhibition at the Marlborough Hotel. We cleaned the Merc and dug out clothes that might do for such an occasion. I glanced at the image of myself in the long wall-mirror in the camp bathroom and thought that the jacket and scarf camouflaged quite well the fact that my trousers were worn and out-moded and that my purple T-shirt had a hole in the sleeve. Bill, who was naturally better presented than me, had managed to scrub up to an acceptable level in a reefer jacket. We drove about three circuits of the town before we found the hotel and then walked into the lounge area to mingle with the well-dressed gathering.

Our illusion of respectability was soon to be shattered. The occasion was accompanied by an abundance of (very good) wine. Because of financial constraints no drop had crossed our lips since we'd drunk that unappealing bottle of Mateus Rosé at the Junction Hotel in Takaka, so this time we seriously overdid it. At some point I became aware that my spine was beginning to dissolve and my voice was coming from some hollow place that didn't seem to have anything to do with me. The woman I was fascinating with my wit began to slip in and out of focus.

'Really,' she kept repeating. 'You don't say.' I watched her mouth pulsating like a blood-red gash in a face that reminded me of uncooked dough.

I sought out Bill in the crowd. He was wavering in front of two women, recounting a story that, perhaps luckily, they seemed incapable of comprehending. His hands were flapping like a pair of protesting pigeons and he laughed robustly, and alone, at his own jokes.

We rescued each other and propelled ourselves with as much dignity as we could muster towards the door. The only sensible thing to do in the circumstances was to leave the car where it was and get a taxi. I poured myself into the front seat. Bill, whose good cheer had turned to gloom, fell into the back.

'Where to?' said the taxi driver, who was round and bald and smelt of mothballs.

'The camping ground,' I replied firmly.

'Which one, love? There are three.'

We hadn't a clue. 'Can we try them all?'

He rolled his eyes and an expression close to pain crossed his face. Precisely one minute later we turned into the Grove Bridge Holiday Park, which we easily recognised. The fare was $2.50. We gave the driver an extra fifty cents, which we hoped would stop him coming back and letting down the tyres of the caravan.

Brave Days and Brass Monkey Nights

Apart from the wine and a mild-mannered taxi man, Blenheim was not at first overwhelming in its welcome. The rain drizzled down and blanketed the place in a milky haze. The camp was close to town but also, we discovered, extremely close to the railway line and the bridge over the river that carried the traffic north to Picton. Heaven could have collapsed on the roof that first night and we would not have woken but after that it was a different story.

Every morning the first train thundered through at five o'clock on its way to the ferry. Its journey began as a distant grating noise but swelled to a roar of avalanche proportions as it approached, shaking the caravan so hard as it passed us that I had to persuade myself it wasn't coming in the door. Then came the high whine of car tyres against the road and the dragon-like hiss of truck engines as they braked for the bend before the bridge. It was like a passing parade from Jurassic Park. There was no hope of earplugs dulling the cacophony and we woke every morning feeling grumpy and tired. Miraculously, after a few weeks we became so used to this extraordinary dawn chorus that we no longer heard it.

The only casual work in Blenheim at that time of the year was boysenberry pruning. Bill enlisted and went off the day after the Day of Monumental Hangovers. Pruning boysenberries was extremely hard work for a fifty-mumble man, even if he was relatively fit. He had to squat on his haunches, holding the cane in his left hand and cutting through the tough thick stalks with his right.

My beloved came home after his first day with 'mutton stare' (a term often used to describe the catatonic state of shearers who have had a hard day). He was still wearing enormous gloves and clutching an evil looking pair of secateurs as if they had become an extension of his hand. His body was bent like a sausage. In Nelson we'd had the great foresight when we bought the new carpet to install underfloor heating in the caravan, and on this he now lay groaning quietly as he tried to straighten himself out.

By the third day the back of his hand had puffed up like a small balloon, but not being the sort of person who lets trivial things get in his way, he stoically stuck at it for two more days by cutting with his left hand. His total pay after tax for such a brave week was something like $185. His next job, painting a friend's outside window frames, was R&R by comparison.

In July it was also becoming very cold at night. Not being a berry pruner, the hardest thing I had to endure was the cold. Some nights the frosts were so heavy and the walls of the caravan so thin that we'd wake up with ice crusting the inside of the windows and our breath exhaling in misty puffs.

We'd become creatures of habit in our sleeping arrangements. The bed lay across the van and I slept on the left next to the outside wall and the window. It was a fair enough arrangement because Bill got up in the night more than I did and it made better sense for me to clamber over him once than for him to clamber over me two or three times. I was not aware of any other disadvantage on my side of the bed – until the weather turned.

The wall against which, if I didn't strongly assert my position, I was pushed became on those brass-monkey nights about the same temperature as the wall on the inside of a freezer. I was terrified I would stick to it if I did not put a wad of blankets between it and the sticking-out bits of my torso.

The loo seats in the ablution blocks were so frigid they made your bowels freeze. One fellow sufferer, June from Gore, who was working in the vineyards, told me that she sang as she sat down. 'It eases the shock,' she said. Forcing myself out of a warm bed, plugging the body into jacket and gumboots and slithering through the frosty grass in the dark to sit on a ring of ice became one of the great physical challenges of the journey. Water sometimes froze in the pipes so, unless we had remembered to save some in a jug, there was no warming cup of tea in the morning.

On other days the clouds were hung out like dirty rags across the sky. When it rained, sometimes steadily for three days on end, we sat it out by experimenting with new recipes, reading, watching television, playing draughts, drinking a lot of wine, going for brave walks in the rain – and every now and then we'd argue.

The worst thing about an altercation in a caravan was that it was hard to introduce any drama to it. I could not sweep from the room and slam the door because there was nowhere to go and anyway it was wet outside. I couldn't sulk extravagantly because we were physically too close, and I couldn't hit him with the cast-iron frying pan because fellow campers would hear his pleas for mercy. The best I could do was to sit there baring my teeth and sticking sharp, preferably barbed, imaginary needles into his vulnerable body parts. I wondered how his mind was dealing with me.

On finer days Bill worked in the vineyards. He started off tying and then pruning, which had to be done with great precision. This was the tough, unglamorous, all-important side of the wine industry. Few of us, when we raised a wine glass of Cloudy Bay Chardonnay or some other liquid delight to our lips, ever thought of the year-round hard slog that went into growing the fruit of the vine – all the hours that were spent in soil preparation, post-hole digging, wiring, grafting, wire dropping, planting, budding, fertilising, stemming, spraying, trimming, de-leafing, watering, disease-monitoring, netting, de-netting, harvesting, pruning and tying. And that was before the grapes got anywhere near a winery.

One thing Bill and I discovered for sure was that, although we would always be happy to drink the end product, we'd never want to own the vines.

Eighteen months later we would return to Blenheim and I'd try my hand at picking grapes for Montana so that I could get out in the fields and be part of the process. It was the year of the drought and the Marlborough Hills, once furry with grass, were bald and smooth. There was a weariness in the land and those hills that had been abused by fire were covered in black and yellow bruises. The trees drooped, the air crackled in the brittle sunlight and the rivers searched across the plains like thirsty tongues.

When I was the *Pacific Wave* editor I had come to Blenheim every year in February for the wine festival and, dressed in fashionable summer robes, had revelled with the crowds in the sunshine, the great food, music and wine. In that milieu grape harvesting sounded rustically romantic – the peasants in the fields rejoicing as they gathered the bounteous offerings of the vine.

I discovered there was absolutely nothing that was romantic about grape picking. Picking on the 18th of March was at Squire Estate on Rapaura Road. I packed sandwiches, sun-block and a water bottle, and reported to the small temporary kiosk at the gate to register. I was given a sheet of stickers with my number on it and a square black bucket, then directed to a bay of vines where I was given a lesson by a cheerfully confident woman called Bunnie who told me she had worked in the vineyards for twenty-seven years.

'First remove some of the leaves which have not been removed by stripping,' she instructed. 'Now hold the bunch of grapes at the bottom end well away from the stalk. Don't allow any leaves to drop into the bucket. Don't drop grapes onto the ground. Leave the second sets, which are those grapes that are hard and bullet-like.'

She handed me the sharpest pair of secateurs I'd ever seen. 'There you go. Have a great day.'

Each row of vines was about 500 metres long and there were about eighty pickers who were each allocated 'bays'. To each bay there were four vines, and our pay was $1 a vine. Pickers moved across the rows, working on one side of a bay and then the other and then moving to the next row. 'We like pickers to keep more-or-less abreast of each other,' Bunnie had said. Quality controllers moved up and down the rows checking that each bay was cleared of grapes – and probably making sure there were no dismembered fingers in the buckets. And they tried to keep everybody happy.

It sounded easy enough but the execution had unexpected pitfalls. It took concentration to fumble around in the protective leaves to look for the stalks, and frequently bunches didn't hang down as they should but gripped around the wires and intertwined so that they were difficult to get at. Being green on green, they were also well camouflaged so that just when I thought I'd cleared a bay, I'd spy another bunch and then another…

After the first hour I was already lagging behind the rest of the field. Barry in the bays adjacent to mine had come from behind and passed me. He worked with pugnacious energy, swearing at the grapes as he went: 'Come 'ere, y'bitch,' or 'Sodding little bugger.' His shoulders bulged from a black woollen singlet and his upper arms were tattooed. A red-and-blue snake wound around his right bicep and on the left was the feathered head of a large eagle. His own head was shaved bare and, as if to compensate, he'd grown a ragged ginger moustache on his upper lip.

As he worked his way past me he told me he'd come up from

Invercargill after being laid off from the smelter. 'It's a bitch, all right. My family's down there but there's no flamin' work. Sodding nothing.'

Barry could do four bays an hour, which worked out at $16. At top speed I could only manage two, and as the day passed my rate dwindled further.

The 'sodding' sun thumped down on my head and after four hours my neck ached and my mind and fingers had gone numb. At intervals along the rows there were collection buckets, into which I was to tip my bucket when it was full. There were two over-stuffed women working next to the collection bucket I used.

'Oi, what do you think you're doin'?' bellowed one. 'Where d'you think we're gonna put our grapes if you put yours there?'

'Get lost,' I ventured weakly. I was too hot to think of a more profound retort.

These two women had what a theatre producer might call 'presence'. For a start their physical being was hard to ignore. Well armoured with flour-bag bosoms and stomachs that had long ago given in to gravity, they were conveyed in a stately manner by sturdy legs and feet encased in well-worn sneakers. They wore floppy hats, and sweaters and water bottles were strapped around what one might once have been referred to as their waists.

But more impressive was the proprietorial dominance they seemed to exert on the field, and their astonishingly rapid progress through the vines. They sailed through their bays like battle-ships, well ahead of the field. These mighty nymphs of Bacchus had been there every year for the past twenty or more, no doubt paying from the proceeds for their kids' education or for holidays or extensions to the kitchen. Despite their rebuff I admired (from a distance) their fortitude and felt like a field mouse by comparison.

In my own character I found very little fortitude: my grape picking days were brief. I worked out that one bottle of Deutz

Méthode Traditionnelle Blanc de Blanc, which was what my pickings would be used for, cost the same amount as my gross pay for four hours' work.

There were better ways to make a living.

Keeping It Simple

Back at the motor camp at Blenheim in the winter of our first year on the road, the place had become sodden and nearly empty. I came to know a group of women from 'down south' who had come there together to find work in the vineyards. They were staying for the winter. In Southland, they said, there was no work to go back to.

David was a single man in his forties. Every morning he cycled 15 kilometres to work in the vineyards and he lived in one of the smallest caravans I had ever seen. He was down on his luck, he told me cheerfully. 'Ah well, it happens, you just have to start again.'

And luck had done nothing for Marcus, who rented a caravan alongside. He was not long out of a two-year prison sentence. He had nowhere to go and struggled to find a job. 'You're never really free when you've served time,' he said. 'I'd like to put my mistakes behind me but other people still see them stickin' out in front.' He took me to see the model farm he was building in his caravan. He was twenty-two, the same age as my son – and I wanted to mother him.

There was still a trickle of travellers: three men from Wyoming who were there to fish the rivers, a bald man in a bus who was travelling with a Siamese cat, a stoical German cyclist who had his worldly goods stuffed into a cart attached to the back of his bike.

These included a minuscule tent shaped like an igloo but undoubtedly not as warm.

And there was Carver, a diminutive man who reminded me of Pinocchio before his nose grew. I'm not sure if the association came from his size or his name. Carver's luck hadn't been too good either.

'I was a jockey once,' he said, grinning to display a gappy row of tea-coloured teeth. His face was also brown and cracked like a walnut shell. 'No nag'll 'ave me now. Too old I reckon. She's sweet, I've always got by. Cosy as a sparrow in a nest I am here.'

Carver lived in a child's play-tent he had purchased from The Warehouse. It was obviously not too waterproof and he'd overcome this by buying two blue tarpaulins, which he had erected over the tent to form two walls and a roof.

'The one thing my dad did for us kids,' he said, 'was teach us how to survive when things got tough.'

Carver had set home-made rabbit snares in the scrubby bush behind the camp and showed me some rather primitive eel traps he'd placed in the sludgy river. To date any wild food had been elusive. He cooked on a small open fire, over which there was a billy on a crossbar. Mostly he cooked fish because he had a mate with a dinghy and they were catching a bit. I took Carver some vegetables from time to time and I noticed other people gave him odds and ends such as tinned tomato, sausages or rice and sometimes cans of beer.

He was a light-hearted little person who, despite his worrying lack of funds, looked as if he was having a lot more fun than a Queen Street sharebroker. He liked to smoke so he looked for fag ends and rolled his own.

'Here, have one,' he said.

I declined.

Carver was allowed to stay in the park provided he kept himself down the far end and didn't use any electricity. On the Sunday after I first met him I walked into the communal kitchen area. Carver was the only other person there. He was absorbed in a feeding frenzy, slurping noisily from a large mug of hot soup and tearing off, with those appalling teeth, great chunks of buttered white toast from a stack on a plate in front of him. He was watching a game of league on the television and he looked like a rat with a gold front tooth. He winked at me. 'Don't tell the bloke in the office. This is my Sunday treat.'

Carver's uncomplicated enjoyment was a life lesson. Bill and I were far from relying on wild rabbits and muddy eels for sustenance, but we struggled to earn enough to keep us going. We were frugal to a cent and many things that once we took for granted, now we savoured – a friend and a good bottle of wine, a latte with a buttered muffin, a movie, a cold beer in a warm bar, an unexpected $5 note in the pocket of a jacket. Oddly, in this new state of poverty we had found such riches. Less was more: I should have remembered that earlier. Never to have too much of anything was one of the most important ingredients of happiness.

We ate very simply. I'd never had a reputation for my culinary repertoire and trying to expand it when the facilities were limited didn't make much sense. In the caravan there was only a two-ring gas stove and a microwave, and occasionally we barbecued outside. We ate grilled meat or fish and plate-loads of winter vegetables, roasted with olive oil, mashed with herbs or lightly boiled. For breakfast we had porridge or muesli and fruit, for lunch leftovers or something like cheese, olives and salami on bread. I came to really enjoy this basic fare and rarely yearned for anything more complex.

The Saturday market in Blenheim was crammed with produce, often excesses from household fruit trees or vegetable gardens. It was reasonably priced, fresh and, if not organic, only lightly sprayed. One of the reasons I was a market junkie was that I could buy straight from the producer without any hype between production and purchase. I could squeeze the lettuce hearts, sniff the tomatoes and poke the aubergines without anyone showing signs of annoyance. And as the stall holder wrapped my purchase in newspaper, I'd often receive a cooking tip or a story. It made limp celery out of supermarket shopping.

One man who grew peppers to fill up the space in between his tomato plants had found they grew so successfully that he and his wife couldn't hope to eat them all. 'Have two for the price of one,' he said. 'These aren't as big as the ones we had last week. We roast them, take off the skins, dip them in olive oil and eat them on toast with a sprinkle of salt and pepper.'

A practical-looking, jolly woman in a print dress and cardigan was selling pots of honey that had been arranged in a pyramid. She explained how she had married a 'bee-man' six years earlier, but before that she 'didn't know a bee from a buffalo'.

She said, 'We've got two hundred hives and we move them around all over the show to different localities for the different types of honey. It's more than a full-time job.' On their stall were lotus major honey (good for the liver), manuka, beech honey dew, blue borage, mixed flower and chicory honey. I tasted the lotus major and bought a jar.

Close by, another woman was offering gourmet rabbit meat and, alongside it, some well-crafted, jointed teddy bears made of rabbit fur. 'Americans love these bears,' she said. 'D'you know that Americans are the biggest bear collectors in the world? They buy them here but we also sell over the net. You'd be amazed at the number of bear collectors there are. I don't know what on earth they do with them.'

I couldn't afford a bear but I left with a mouse, which sat on a ledge in the caravan for about a year. It ended its tenancy when we were visiting a friend in Greymouth who lamented that for a whole week he'd caught no rats in the trap he'd set under his house. Next morning he reported the capture of a rabbit-skin mouse.

I loved the market for its social aspect, which was often pure theatre. A small, neat octogenarian in a white bowling hat and navy track-suit sat in a deck chair in the sun behind a table of home-knitted babies' booties and bibs, satin hearts, tea cosies, knitted slippers and mittens, and dolls dressed in layers of lace. A friend of hers had stopped for a chat. She was a larger women with false teeth that every now and then she stirred with her tongue. 'He did, you know,' I heard her say. 'Went right up to her and…' I couldn't catch the end of the sentence but the two women whinnied with laughter.

Next to the Four Paws pet-food van was the fresh fish van: 'We catch our own'. The slim Maori girl in attendance was eating a hot dog on a stick and reading a magazine. On the wall behind her sat three men in their eighties, with their shirt sleeves rolled up and wearing identical floppy brown hats on their heads, presumably waiting for their wives. Unmoving and in silence they watched the pageant before them. Squatting like a garden ornament at the feet of the middle man, a small Jack Russell dog stared in the same direction. He didn't have a floppy hat.

Unlike at the Nelson market, there was not a lot of artistic showcasing or local musical talent. One busker, a skinny adolescent boy in shorts playing a flute, had a cardboard notice on the pavement at his feet, next to a man's upturned felt hat. 'I would like to continue music lessons,' it read, hopefully. 'Can you help?' I gave him a couple of dollars for boldness. I would never have had the confidence to do that in my teens.

Apart from Southland swedes and outdoor peppers, my greatest culinary conversion and subsequent addiction in Marlborough was to freshly pressed extra-virgin olive oil. It happened on one crisp, clear day when I was lounging on the patio of Triska Blumenfeld's harbourside home outside Picton. A cluster of bright white yachts tugged at their moorings just beyond us, a few ducks slid quietly past at the bottom of the garden, and we ripped hunks of crispy bread off baguettes, dipped them into warm bowls of oil that was 'straight off the press' and dabbed them into Maldon salt flakes. The oil was silky in texture and had a faint aroma of freshly cut grass and a lemony taste as pure and irresistible as early-morning sunshine. Eaten between sips of cool Sauvignon Blanc from Gillan Estate, seduction was inevitable.

Triska's own enchantment had taken place years earlier. She had succumbed not only to the subtleties of the good oil but also to the charms of the man who was to become the pioneer of olive growing in New Zealand. When in his wife's native land he first saw the dry hills of Marlborough, the late Israeli horticulturist Gidon Blumenfeld dreamed of covering them in olive trees. Throughout the Mediterranean the tastes and health benefits of olive oil had been enjoyed for centuries, but when Gidon came to New Zealand it was better known as Popeye's girlfriend than as an ingredient of a healthy cooking style.

Triska spoke softly in slow, considered sentences that matched the elegant way she was dressed. 'In 1986 we planted a grove of olive trees near Blenheim to raise stock for propagating and selling,' she said. 'By 1990 we had twenty cultivars in our grove and in 1991, just before Gidon died, we imported the first commercial oil press into New Zealand.'

Triska had continued her love affair with oil even though she was no longer involved in the growing or production. 'I rub it over my body before I have a shower,' she said, 'and use it as a moisturiser for my face and hands.' I looked at my own red and wrinkled paws next to her smooth, pale ones and determined that from now on I would lather myself in oil. But, like a lot of other tasks of body maintenance, I never got around to it.

There was something special about eating and drinking close to the source of things like olive oil and wine. It was partly because in areas where climate and geography had conspired to create good conditions for growing grapes and olive trees, they often created great scenery as well. Around Blenheim, food and wine writers and some excellent chefs had helped to forge the images that portrayed Marlborough as a romantic Utopia.

Visitors to the district came to sit beneath sun umbrellas among the vines, where they quaffed the best vintages and consumed platefuls of scallops and salmon, hors d'oeuvres of pâté, gherkins, olives and artichoke hearts, or mains of spinach, pumpkin and sun-dried tomato frittata, topped with ragout and grilled bacon. They mopped up the juices with thick-crusted bread, rinsed their palates with a last glass of wine and sank into a post-prandial torpor that could last all afternoon.

Sitting under a caravan awning with a plate of Southland swede, even if it was roasted in olive oil, didn't have quite the same ring to it. And so Bill and I, just once, took ourselves off to lunch with the hedonists. At a table in the small, sheltered courtyard of the Cairnbrae Vineyards restaurant on Jacksons Road I polished off a rosy medallion of cold roast beef with a glistening green salad and a chutney made of mango and peaches. Bill had smoked sausage made into a salad with cheese, pickled gherkins, small red onions, tomato and mustard. We drank a bottle of Old River Riesling and celebrated our good fortune at having discovered life on the road. And we felt maniacally joyous at the thought that the meal had cost us three days' budget.

Next to us was a French family – three teenage sons, an older girl and mother and father – who punctuated their consumption of an ample meal and several bottles of wine with discernible phrases such as 'bon appétit' and 'à votre santé' and, 'Merci, le repas est délicieux,' and, 'Ou sont les toilettes, s'il vous plait?' If I'd closed my eyes, I could have been back in the Loire Valley or in a courtyard café in Provence. It occurred to me that I would just as soon be in Marlborough.

Not the Whole Hog

When people knew we were on the move we were quite often offered the use of their house while they were on holiday. It was a good two-way arrangement: the house was cared for and we got to weave our way into the local community, rest from the dislocation and uncertainties of being on the road and spread out in a space that was considerably larger that 13 square metres.

I had cut my house-sitting teeth many years earlier near a tiny village in Northland called Ohaeawai. My friends Chris and Sam Ludbrook lived in a large two-storeyed landmark house built of timber. It was surrounded by a sizeable chunk of land that rolled away to distant hummocky hills. I had my three children with me then, and each morning Rachel and Inge set off across the damp, lumpy paddocks and clambered over the dry-stone walls to go to Ohaeawai School, which had a roll of about twenty pupils.

My role, I had decided, was as a kind of farmer's wife but without the farmer. I'd not had much practice.

'It'll be fine,' Sam assured me. 'There's nothing to do really but if you have any problems call the neighbour. Her name is Edith. Oh, and if the pigs get in the vegie garden,' Chris added, 'just grab the pig buckets from the kitchen and call, "Here piggy piggy piggy," and walk towards the gate. They'll follow you, no problem.'

They made a few other muffled reassuring noises and

disappeared down the driveway in a stationwagon loaded with luggage. From the swirls of dust that almost hid them from view came joyous toots of departure.

It was spookily quiet when they had gone. The six working dogs, which were now in my charge, gave me no confidence. Chained to their kennels, all six sat on their haunches gazing forlornly after the car. The two house cats, Lucy and Zoe, wound hopefully around my legs.

At about six o'clock on our second night there the phone went. 'You lookin' after Ludbrooks'?' said a laconic male voice on the other end.

'Er, yes.'

'Well, your bulls are on the road. Couple of 'em. Saw them just now. Better get that fixed pronto, I reckon.'

I rang Edith.

'Yep, okay,' she said in a tone that rang with the efficiency of a commando officer. 'I'll get the boys onto it.' The boys were two young stock agents who had sold Sam the bulls in the first place and for some reason still had some sort of responsibility. Ten minutes later Edith appeared, not on a white charger, but on an old tractor that belched and farted all the way up the drive.

'You'd better offer the boys a feed,' she bellowed above the din. 'They'll have an appetite by the time they've finished.' She drove off to oversee proceedings.

Of course that's what they did in the country – always had mountains of food for callers and unexpected happenings. My fridge was alarmingly bare. I put the children on half rations and organised two plates of chicken with salad and potatoes and peas. Pleased with my rural resourcefulness, I covered them with tea-towels and left them on the bench.

It took two hours for the bulls to be reinstated in the front paddock and for the fence they had knocked over to be roughly mended. I did not have a powerful presence in the proceedings but when the boys came to the house to say they had finished I did my bit.

'Would you boys like some dinner?' I said in capable, farm-wifely tones.

'Oh, yeah, great, I reckon,' they chorused enthusiastically.

I led them to the kitchen and there upon the bench was mayhem. Lucy and Zoe, ever the opportunists, had with feline cunning beaten them to it and all that remained were some scattered peas and tattered bits of lettuce. I didn't know that cats ate potato. Out the kitchen window I could see Lucy's black ears twitching behind a cabbage in the vegie patch. I hoped she was throwing up.

I gave the boys two stiff tots of Sam's whisky instead and they went away bemused but well pleased.

The three-week stay at Ohaeawai was crammed with events. One wet and windy day I called the local vet to tend to a limping horse, a big bay mare who looked as if she was in great pain. The leg hung loosely from her shoulder and every time she put it to the ground she looked as if she was about to tumble forward onto her nose. When the vet finally arrived I was horrified to see that he was hobbling almost as badly as the horse. He gave me a bashful glance and then, with averted eyes, pulled up his right trouser leg to show me a knee that was the size and colour of a football. He'd been kicked, he told me, and had applied horse liniment to the injury. It had crisped the skin around the joint like barbecued chicken.

It was raining hard. We squelched across three soggy paddocks to reach the afflicted mare. She must have feared the final bullet because she galloped off across the paddock on three legs so efficiently that, in half an hour of trying, we were unable to catch her. The vet hobbled wetly back to his car muttering like a man gone mad. I didn't enquire as to the content.

There were other things too but nothing quite so dramatic as the day of pigs. I looked out the kitchen window on a bright and sunny morning and there in the vegetable patch were six bulky pink sows, their ears flopping rhythmically as they ripped the cabbages from their stalks and rooted with their snouts among the beetroot. I screamed for the children.

'What we do,' I said, parroting my instructions, 'is each take a pig bucket (there were four) and walk across the lawn to the gate calling "Here piggy piggy piggy," and then we drop the contents of the buckets outside the gate when the pigs have followed. It's quite simple.'

We began the manoeuvre. One 'Here piggy' and half a tonne of pork, uttering loud predatory grunts, came trotting at speed. And to this day I am ashamed to have to confess that I was the first to drop my bucket and run for the fence. The three children, who looked to me for guidance and perhaps valour in the face of danger, followed suit. Their squealing outrivalled the pigs' but, with their greater speed, they vaulted to safety well before I did.

So there we were on the outside of the garden, with the pigs still inside, smugly wolfing the contents of four pig buckets.

I rang Edith.

Towards the end of our stay in Blenheim Toni Gillan called in to the caravan for morning coffee. With her husband she owned and ran Gillan Estate Wines on Rapaura Road. I had known them for a long time.

'I've a favour to ask,' she said. 'Terry and I are off to England for a month and we were hoping you and Bill could stay in the house and keep an eye on things. It might suit you to have a break.'

It did indeed. The winter was hanging in. The weather hadn't improved and we were beginning to develop cabin fever.

From an architectural point of view, Gillan Estate was one of the most impressive wine buildings in the district. Classy, bold, white and Mediterranean in style, it had a sizeable hangar-shaped cellar at the front and, behind this and attached to it, a thoroughly

modern home. The building was sited on a piece of land on Rapaura
Road among an orchard of cherry trees and 5 hectares of Pinot
and Chardonnay grapes.

So there we were, from the ridiculous to the sublime, surrounded
by 55,000 fermenting bottles of méthode traditionnelle, and living
the life of Riley. We were also guardians of Marley, a Labrador
dog. Marley too was thoroughly modern – a girl with a mind of
her own. She took me for walks through the naked vines and
dripping cherry trees in the watery winter sun. I wondered if this
was like living in Tuscany in winter.

Marley also liked to wander to neighbouring properties and,
because her predecessor was run over on Rapaura Road, I spent
half my day chasing her and pleading with her to come home. It
was a futile pursuit. She completely ignored my presence as she
went about the doggy business of hunting out rabbits and skinks
and canine companions. If I came within grabbing distance of her
collar she would throw me a disdainful glance and amble off just
out of reach. It was, I supposed, one way to keep fit. Another was
to lock Marley in the house and walk alone along the willow-
covered bank of the Opawa River, which swirled not far from the
road, or trudge up the limb-testing Wither Hills behind the town.

Working among the vines was keeping Bill trim, and he'd
developed a dusky tan as if he'd been working outdoors all his life.
He had moved from pruning to dropping wires, which required
him to walk up to 14 kilometres a day down the rows of vines, and
at each post reach up to lift the wire off a nail and then bend down
to clip it under a nail at the bottom. The wires had been put on top
of the post by the pruners and had to be lowered again so that the
new growth had something to grab on to. Then they were
progressively lifted up the posts as the vine grew. Wire droppers
were paid one-and-a-half cents per plant, which was six cents a
post. On a long day Bill might de-wire up to 2000 posts. So he
was bringing home the bacon – but not the whole hog.

Much of what he earned went back into his own refuelling. Each morning he made himself eight sandwiches, huge enough to challenge the oral capacity of a horse, packed bananas, apples and biscuits, and headed off for the vineyards with a large lunch box and a water bottle tucked under his arm. By lunch time he'd already eaten four of the sandwiches and much of the fruit. By the time he got home at five-thirty he needed stoking with a southern man's menu – two cans of Speight's, a large piece of steak and half a sack of potatoes.

The house at Gillan Estate was outfitted with the sort of amenities we had come to regard as super luxurious – spa bath, giant bed, double fridge and freezer, huge oven, double sink and Wastemaster and ensuite bathrooms. In this house I could go from loo to shower to bed without once putting on my gumboots. Every time I felt a tingle of pleasure. It reminded me that, to be of any value, things must be weighed against their opposite. At home it had never crossed my mind that inside amenities could be such a treat.

S taying in someone else's home territory gave us an entrée into local life and we took up with some of the Gillans' friends. Every few days Roz Warner would bobble up the driveway in her plum-and-custard coloured Citroën 2CV. 'My motorised pram,' she called it. Roz was the winery cook and in summer produced tapas and other fine dishes for the sybarites who came to gorge themselves on long lunches and wine out in the courtyard, and play idle games of pétanque under the cherry trees.

She was renowned in Blenheim for her enormous chocolate cakes, which she dubbed Black Magic, and for paella. Her seafood paella was so sought-after that one of her paella-dinners-for-twenty was auctioned at the charity Winter Wine Auction held at the Cloudy Bay winery. It went for $1000. The prize was offered up under the trees in Roz's garden out on Hawkesbury Road. Not being one of the favoured twenty, I could only salivate as she recounted how she rattled up the enormous rice dish in a paella pan over an open fire. We were drinking coffee at the time, in her tiny, whitewashed, two-room cob cottage, which had been built in 1847.

'How long ago did you buy this?' I said, looking around at the teeny-weeny, dim interior with its cram of furniture, its tapestry cushions and pot-belly stove, and wondering how she could cope with the lack of space. Living at the winery I'd forgotten that two of us usually lived in a space that was quite a lot smaller than this.

'Oh, I haven't bought it, I rent it,' she said. 'It was an old shepherd's shelter in the time when they used to drive great flocks of sheep from Nelson through Molesworth Station to Canterbury.'

The afternoon was cooling and Roz lit the fire. I went out to stow my bag, a large piece of Black Magic and some cold paella in the car and glanced back at the cottage. Against a backdrop of dark trees smoke was wafting up from the chimney. It was just the sort of place where Little Red Riding Hood might have come to visit her grandma.

The winery was closed at that time of the year. But there was a wedding held in the cellar, which, even though it was lined with large quantities of the demon drink, had a chapel-like quality about it. The wine was stacked in walled cells on either side of a cavernous central space. At the far end two imposing wooden doors opened from a wide tree-lined driveway into the cellar and at the other end, next to the kitchen, was a curved bar which served equally well as an altar. For the wedding, to which we were invited because we were there, the whole space was bedecked with bows and flowers. And we sat on rows of wooden benches facing the bar.

The bride and her entourage made an eye-catching entrance through the double doors, accompanied by a timely burst of sunshine. After the marriage ceremony the benches were replaced by long trestle tables, and a feast of smoked salmon fritatta, pan-fried potatoes and gourmet sausages appeared from the kitchen. It was accompanied by the cellar's best traditionnelle. When the feasting was over the tables were removed and the music turned up, and we danced in the echoing space of the cellar until two in morning.

As the Gillans' house sitters we were also invited across the road to the Le Brun Family Estate winery for the launch of Daniel Le Brun's new méthode traditionnelle. About forty people had gathered by invitation in the winery and were treated to the first public tasting of this rather good vintage of bubbles, along with some pastries and sandwiches.

Daniel and his wife had a long history in the district as producers of some very fine méthode traditionnelle wines. Daniel was a champenois, from a family of French champagne makers going back twelve generations. Looking for wider horizons he emigrated to New Zealand in 1975, first setting up Cellier Le Brun and later shifting to a new winery on Rapaura Road. This was the first vintage from the new winery.

They called it No. 1, which I felt rather lent itself to being dubbed 'Daniel's piss'. But, in an area of the country where wine was taken very seriously, if anybody else had made the connection they were too polite to mention it – and so was I.

Racing and Rollers

About a month after we left Gillan Estate, Jamie Gordon, who lived near Ashburton, rang to say that he and his wife Mel were off to America for three weeks and would we like to stay in the house. They lived about 15 kilometres outside the town near the Five Star Beef feedlot where Jamie worked.

We'd not considered Ashburton as a destination but it was an opportunity to spend time in mid-Canterbury and I thought perhaps I'd grow to like it. I'd never found much to love about the Canterbury Plains. There was nothing to hold me there, no anchoring hills or intriguing forests, no hidden corners to surprise me. All straight lines and intensive agriculture, intercepted only by the wide curving paths of stranded rivers that tumbled from the distant Alps and wandered stonily to the ocean.

After three weeks of living just outside Ashburton nothing much happened to change my mind. The countryside was so flat I thought I could lie in the middle of a paddock of wheat stubble and see the horizon, although I never actually tried this. But I liked the sense of space created by the great dome of an uninterrupted sky – a huge canvas on which the elements etched their intent and some evenings, as the sun went down, flushed the undersides of whipped-cream clouds a glorious neon pink.

Jamie rented the house he had lent us and at that freezing time of year it was rather cold and draughty, but we had electric blankets on the bed, which we didn't have in the caravan. We were early to bed and late to rise, amusing ourselves by reading. I developed a technique that allowed all of my person, apart from my head, two fingers, a thumb and part of my hand (which held the book) to remain snugly under the duvet. I borrowed a woollen beanie for my head. I was warm but according to my beloved any form of romance was out of the question.

At night the temperature was several degrees below zero, the water pipes froze and glittering frost stiffened the grass and sometimes didn't melt until mid-afternoon. Anything left outside overnight developed severe rigor mortis. Inside, the house would not be warmed. Bill lit the fire in the lounge each morning but the heat dissipated before it reached any other part of the room. All it did was set up a draught that moaned under the door and set our teeth on edge.

Still, it was quiet and many degrees warmer than it would have been in the caravan. I found the best way of coping was to quit my own moaning, pull a woolly hat over my head, don the warmest jacket I could find among the thicket of garments hanging in the washhouse, shove my hands in its pockets and front up to the elements. Bill preferred to burrow into his sleeping bag and sit hopefully in front of the fire. He looked like a large red caterpillar.

I became quite fond of the town, which had a comfortable, well-ordered air and some nice surprises. At the Regent, for instance, you could sit at the back of the theatre at one of two formica tables, order up a steak from Cactus Jacks next door and eat your dinner while you watched the movie. I wasn't sure how you would find your mouth in the gloom and suspected that a few peas and trimmed bits of fat would end up down the neck of a traditionally seated movie-goer. Still the idea held the possibility of a different night out.

Ashburton hadn't tried to outdo itself. It just was what it was – a country service town which was buoyant when farming was booming and subdued when it wasn't. Life there seemed cheerful and uncomplicated, even though the townsfolk sometimes displayed anxiety when they sought, in barely disguised terms, our opinion of the district. 'Great place,' they'd say and then look at us suspiciously, as if they were waiting for us to deny it. 'Here for a few weeks then? So what d'you think so far?' or, 'Think you'll stay on at all?'

Shop attendants were obliging and friendly, and people took a personal interest in our well-being. I went to a clothing store in the main street to buy a pair of knickers. 'Try them on,' said the cuddly looking sales girl. 'I always try them on. There's nothing worse than tight ones and you can't change them. They cost enough.' I wasn't quite sure if this was a kind of Brer Rabbit sales technique or whether she was genuinely trying to put me off.

I dutifully retired to a cubicle behind a blue curtain. The knicker girl hovered outside and after a decent pause to allow me time to get things in place she asked companionably, 'How're you doing?' And offered a bit of advice: 'Make sure they're not cutting your privates.'

I was charmed into buying two pairs.

Not all customers were quite as satisfied, it seemed. I was in a supermarket when a pugnacious-looking middle-aged man in a dark blue boiler suit lost his rag.

'Think this is f—ing service do ya, ya fat slugs?' he hollered from the doorway. 'Youse couldn't serve a f—ing pig, especially that f—ing cow behind the counter!'

As the verbal explosion resounded through the aisles of baked beans and creamed corn, the soap powders and fruit stalls, twenty shoppers froze as if a video was on pause. I would have thought that in a brawny country town someone would have shown a bit of muscle, but no one raced up and punched the man on the nose or shouted at him to 'Piss off' or 'Get lost, dickhead' or even 'Mind your language'. When he'd left, the video restarted and everybody carried on as if the event had never occurred. The only reaction was that of the young, gentle-looking 'cow' behind the counter, whose face had gone self-deprecatingly pink.

One of the things that really impressed me all over the country was the inventiveness that went on in backyards. There were people who built their own lavender crushers, replica cars and solar-powered bicycles, who restored steam tractors and vintage aircraft, and built mini observatories and furniture, and designed water pumps and dog gumboots – and the highest accolade they got from their neighbours was a mention in passing: 'Oh yes, that's Fred. He's a clever bloke,' or, 'That's sounds like Jim. He's the fellow who made that gizmo that's used all over the world.'

My curiosity was aroused when I read an article in the local paper extolling the skills of a man called Bruce McIlroy, who had a Rolls-Royce workshop. I thought that in the unlikely event of my ever owning a Roller he might be a man worth knowing. What was a home-town Ashburton boy doing as one of only two accredited Rolls-Royce mechanics in the country? He had to be extraordinary to be visited by the top brass of the Rolls-Royce headquarters from Crewe, in England, and be invited to join the select band of accredited mechanics. Such a vote of confidence was a high accolade. That it was given to a man in a workshop in the backyard of a modest home on the rural fringes of Ashburton was heady stuff.

I imagined Bruce to be a soft-skinned urbanite in a pin-striped suit and with manicured nails and black hair slicked back with Brylcreem. In reality he was a tall, rugged man with an outdoor complexion, who looked as if he might have come in from working his dogs or checking the fences – except that he wore immaculately clean grey overalls with RR and B logos embroidered on the pocket.

He affected a casual manner but I suspected he was highly organised. He'd have to be. Bill and I were escorted around the workshop, which was a large shed of corrugated iron that had none of the greasy, dusty turmoil of most male domains. The yard outside was swept clean. The interior was as organised as a dental surgery: the polished tools hung immaculately according to size and use, the diagnostic equipment was neatly stored, the library of reference books and CD-ROMs was as orderly as an army on parade. Under shrouds of white cloth to keep off the dust, two dignified older Bentleys were perched on blocks awaiting disembowelment. There was not one mucky drop of grease in sight.

'I service thirty to forty cars a year,' Bruce told us, reverently pulling back the shroud of a Silver Ghost (actually painted cream) so that we could admire its fine lines and polished surfaces. The gesture contained all the care of a man pulling back a coverlet to reveal his sleeping son.

'Some of them need total mechanical rebuilds,' he said. 'Other jobs can be pretty complex. There's nothing simple about a Rolls engine; even old ones were incredibly sophisticated for their time. There's always a waiting list.'

'So what've you got at the moment?' said Bill, who was salivating not so much at the cars but at the size of the work shed that contained them. Then, without waiting for the answer, he turned to me and said, 'If we ever settle down again I'd like a shed like this.'

In his dreams.

At the moment,' said Bruce, 'I've got three Bentley turbos, a Silver Shadow and a Silver Cloud, two Silver Ghosts and a Bentley Continental R.'

Bill nodded in a clubby sort of way. It didn't mean much to me. They were fine-looking machines whatever they were called.

Bruce couldn't remember a time when he wasn't interested in machines. His first memory of hands-on experience was when he was eight and he dismantled the family motor mower to see how it worked and then put it together again. Nine years later when he left school he didn't have to think twice about a career path.

'I qualified as an A-grade mechanic when I was twenty-two,' he said, rubbing his hand over the flank of the Bentley Continental R. 'And I bought my first Bentley when I was eighteen. A few years later I bought a Phantom III and by then I'd learnt enough to completely rebuild its engine.'

His penchant for Rolls-Royce and Bentley engines became well established and so did his reputation as an excellent mechanic who understood the elegant engineering of Rolls and Bentley cars. Owners started to seek him out. Some sent their cars to Ashburton by train; one even sent a Rolls from the North Island by Hercules. Now, he said, he knew every nut, bolt and bracket that hung these cars together and understood the complexities, idiosyncrasies and engineering style of every Rolls-Royce engine since Henry Royce rolled out the first model in 1904.

I n Ashburton we also kept hearing the name of Lindsay Kerslake, a man who owned a trotting-horse stud and training centre near Lauriston and had invented a kind of tandem sulky so that visitors to the stud could race a trotter or pacer with a trained driver sitting beside them. I rang his house and his wife Jan answered. She'd been the guinea pig for that prototype tandem and gave it a resounding endorsement. So one day I bullied Bill into taking me out there. Bill didn't go in for horses much.

'That first time I got behind a horse was awesome,' Jan said when we arrived at the farm. 'I was so enthusiastic we went ahead and had the first six sulkies made and now hundreds of people have experienced what I did.'

Bill and I were about to join them. Togged in rather fetching red-and-purple racing silks, a helmet and enormous goggles – a vision that would have made any sensible horse bolt – I slid into the sulky behind a huge red mare called Moose (her racing name was Talk About Me). I was grateful to have Lindsay there beside me. I'd ridden horses since I was ten years old, but this was very different. The horse was way out in front with only the reins for communication. It crossed my mind that, if she wanted to, Moose could head for the hills, spilling us onto the track and reducing the flimsy sulky to splinters, and there wasn't much we could do to stop her. She was no old nag but a woman with a reputation in the world of harness racing. She'd won a lot of money in her day.

As an observer I'd always been enthralled by harness horses sprinting around a track – the way the thudding hooves and whirring wheels surged close, thundered past and faded. But being the one holding the reins behind all that thrusting horsepower as it reached speeds of up to 50 kilometres per hour was an idea that had more than the horses racing.

Lindsay gave me the reins and a few warm-up laps settled my palpitations. Bill was whizzing along behind a smaller black horse, but I was so focused on keeping Moose in a good mood I didn't really have time to look at him. When the horses were turned to the starting line they pricked up their ears and picked up their pace. Lindsay only had to shout 'Go!' and they were racing. The surge of power was incredible. For the next four minutes it was all flying grit, drumming hooves and heavy breathing. Bill's mare pounded up behind us and stayed there, blowing great hot explosions down my neck. And then just before the post she pipped us, squeezing past so close I thought we'd lock wheels.

'Can't win 'em all,' said Lindsay, as he pulled Moose back to a jog.

'Awesome,' was all I could manage.

Back at our accommodation Jamie and Mel had returned from America. Jamie carted us off to look over the feedlot. I had just finished reading *My Year of Meat* by Ruth Ozeki, which made me feel a little queasy about any form of flesh, but Five Star Beef had a different set-up from the one described in the book.

Jamie drove us around, explaining as we went. 'These are brought here for about two hundred and sixty days and fattened,' he said, pointing to pens that contained the bulky and placid presence of Angus and Angus/Hereford cattle. The beasts gazed at us with large, brown, contented eyes as we drove past.

We turned a corner and stopped outside a high shed that contained piles of feed. A front-end loader was scooping into the heaps and transferring portions of them to the tray of a truck. Most of this fodder was grown on the country around Ashburton.

'It's a bit like a resort holiday,' I said. 'All that food…'

A girl rode past on a horse. Twice a day she did the rounds of the 15,000 or so animals to check on their health and happiness. Apparently disease was rare.

'In summer,' said Jamie, 'the animals are cooled by the sea breezes which funnel up over that cliff there. They're survival-oriented so as long as they have enough to eat and drink and a comfortable space they're happy.'

It was also a happy thing that they had no knowledge of what lay ahead. When they reached the required weight they would be taken away to the meatworks and slaughtered, and their ample flesh packed and chilled and sent to Japan. When I thought about it, none of us knew what lay ahead. I wondered what would eventually become of my own ample flesh.

A Seal of Love

We travelled to Kaikoura to catch up with friends we'd met in Nelson who had been circuiting New Zealand for eight years in a large Bedford bus. They phoned to say they had broken down in Hanmer Springs and couldn't make it for another week. One of the things I liked about this wayward life was the *laissez faire* attitude of relationships. The camaraderie was easy come, easy go. If it happened, that was fine. If it didn't, that was fine. It was a relief after the anxiety of my old appointment-driven lifestyle, which often held such energy-sapping obligation.

We told Sue and Tom we'd stay a while in Kaikoura and catch them in Hanmer if they were still there in a week or so. 'See y'on the road,' I said – roadie vernacular for 'Let's catch up sometime.'

Kaikoura had a strong personality. The jagged peaks of the seaward mountain range jabbed at the sky and loomed over the gigantic desolation of an angry ocean to give the place an air of melodrama. The town itself looked accidental and temporary, as if the forces of such a powerful environment could have wiped it off the map at any moment. It could be a melancholy place when the sun was not out. At night, if I stood alone on the shore, the wind keened in off the sea in a despairing lament that tingled the back of my neck and sent me scuttling back to the lights of the town and the security of the caravan.

. . .

We'd set up in the Beach Road Holiday Park on the main road into town. The washroom there, like washrooms all over the country, was a meeting ground. There was something companionable about going about daily body-cleaning rituals with complete strangers. Teeth-cleaning in unison had a kind of unspoken intimacy. There was a wide variety of styles in the pursuit of dental hygiene. In communal bathrooms from the north to the south I watched nodders, waggers, scrubbers and suckers, swallowers, spitters, wavers, pretenders and flossers. Face-cleansing produced dabbers, scrapers, polishers, foamers, sloshers and lick-and-promisers.

At Kaikoura, between toothpaste smiles and soapy introductions, I befriended two girls from Germany. They had pitched their tent over the hedge from where we were parked, displaying Teutonic resilience in the face of the haunting wind. Claudia and Petra had become besotted by the dolphins that roamed the sea around Kaikoura. They'd been whale watching too, but it was the dolphins that caught their fancy. Every morning they disappeared to go dolphin spotting or dolphin swimming and they came back around midday with love shining from their eyes.

'Dat vas da best thing we've done in the whole time we've been in Nu Zealand,' Claudia told me.

I really liked Claudia. She was probably in her early thirties, no chit of a girl but a woman of very generous proportions with a chortling sense of humour. She was the most comprehensive abluter I had ever come across. It could be an hour's entertainment to be with Claudia in the washroom. I could tell it was her in the shower when I walked into the room and great waves of strawberry soap scent were wafting steamily out of one of the cubicles. Ten minutes later she would emerge clad in a towel that, around her ample body, looked more like a face flannel. She looked like a Rubenesque nymphette. In full public view she would massage her voluminous flesh with two types of moisturiser. Next, she lavished her armpits with a deodorant that smelt of apples and sprayed a rose-scented perfume on her neck and forearms. Then she disappeared back into her cubicle and emerged a few minutes later fully dressed and smelling like a flower garden.

The next phase was to don a scarf-like band around her hair, line up five or six pots, tubes and bottles on the ledge in front of the mirror and proceed to rub or pat their contents on various parts of her face and neck. She was methodical. No container was opened until the last one had its cap screwed back in place. Then, with studied concentration, Claudia began what my mother would have called 'putting on her face'. Again this involved a shelf of containers and much rubbing and slapping and drawing, and in between each layer she peered at the result with obvious satisfaction. Miraculously the end result was not the look of a vaudeville clown but of natural and glowing good health. While all this was going on I couldn't, of course, stare at her so I busied myself with splashings and pattings of my own.

Claudia was not one to be fooled. She snapped shut the catch of her enormous toilet case, turned to me and said with an eyelashy wink, 'Beauty is in ze eye of ze beer holder.' She was, I noticed, partial to a pint or two.

Even in the vast arena of the ocean no dolphin could have missed Claudia's perfumed presence on her morning swims. I'd also swum with dolphins and enjoyed the experience but I felt I had more affinity with seals. When Bill played golf I would take myself off to sit with the colony that lived just past the twin tunnels on the road south from the town. A group stretched out languidly on the rocks like forty overweight mermaids. They lolled about, stretching and yawning with lazy self-indulgence, peering at me occasionally, half curiously and half anxiously, with huge, dripping, brown eyes. These cosy creatures could wrench endearments from the most hard-hearted human, but one great bewhiskered yawn displaying

JILL MALCOLM

long spiky mustard-coloured fangs and emanating the stink of
rotten fish put love to the test. And all that cute, hug-me demeanour
could also quickly evaporate if you happened to get between a seal
and the water.

When they took to the water the seals were marvellous to watch.
A bit of floating driftwood would turn out to be a seal lolling on
its back, holding its flippers up as if it were Claudia examining her
fingernails. Another might be on its side, resting with a single
flipper held aloft, and then suddenly it would start rolling sideways,
over and over, and splashing joyously.

I agonised for them when they dragged themselves from the
water. All their agility was gone. They dipped their heads, strained
against their front flippers and galumphed their blubbery bodies
over the sharp rocks like shipwrecked sailors hauling themselves
ashore with their last gasp. When they flopped down to rest, their
whole bodies collapsed like sacks of dough. No wonder they were
rather ill-tempered with their mates, hissing at any that might
challenge their rock, and showing those formidable teeth.

I went swimming with them once in the churning, eerie, emerald
world just off the rocks. Water temperatures were icy. A small
group of us, togged in double wetsuits and guided by local seal-
swimming operator Graeme Chambers, waddled like Michelin
men across the stony foreshore to the edge of the water. There
were not many seals lying up at that time of the year. Most of
them were out at sea, chasing squid to plump up their fat layers.
But the stop-at-homes slipped into the water soon after we did
and approached us cautiously.

I was flailing around in a forest of bull kelp, rapidly building up
an oxygen debt, when the first large female skimmed silently
beneath me. I saw her quite clearly. Effortlessly she rolled full circle,
keeping one eye on me and then the other. I marvelled at her
ability to flow through that foreign environment as if she herself
were made of liquid. No need to ask who was at home there.

'In the summer there are up to six hundred seals on the rocks in this area,' Graeme said. 'So far they have treated visitors very nicely but you should keep your head down. If you raise it too high it could be seen as a challenge.'

I kept mine so low after that I was in danger of drowning.

'It's kinda curious,' he said, 'that when snorkellers enter the water around here a few female and adolescent seals always leave the males to grumble over territory and slip quietly into the water to investigate. They really seem to enjoy the company.'

As we returned to shore one of the five females who had joined us followed. I felt sure I was the chosen one. She ducked and spun and spy-hopped around me, making contact with her huge beseeching eyes. And she hovered in the water for a few minutes near the place where we clambered out onto the rocks.

Later that evening I told Claudia that she would have no competition for dolphin affections from me. I was in love with a seal.

It was a similar feeling for an animal that led me to visit Nikki and John Smith's farm some way out of Kaikoura, which was reached by a tortuous shingle driveway about 6 kilometres in length. As I pulled up in the yard beside the house they both came out to see who had arrived. I didn't think they would remember me.

'Well hello,' they said in unison. 'It's been a long time.'

'About four years,' I said.

'The last time I heard of you was a while ago. You were travelling around in a caravan,' Nikki said.

'Still am,' I said.

I'd first met Nikki and John a few years earlier when I'd undertaken a trek on horseback that started in Kaikoura, crossed the Seaward Kaikoura Range to follow the Clarence River through to Molesworth Station and ended up in Hanmer Springs. It was a ride of some ten days guided by Rob Stanley from Hurunui, and was one of the toughest and most magnificent I have done in a lifetime of riding horses. The Smiths had penned the horses after the first day's five-hour ride, and had provided our first night of accommodation.

They were friendly, open and very hospitable people and I was looking forward to seeing them, but just as strong a reason for driving out of town was the thought that I might meet up with Tacker, the lion-hearted mare I had ridden on the trek. She was a tall, bold, black horse bred in the high country on St James Station, which was well known for its rearing of brave and sturdy horses. Out there St James horses had status.

Tacker taught me a lot about living. She had stamina, courage, enthusiasm, good manners and a kind of spiritual toughness. She went places I would have left to the goats – scrambling up narrow ledges and skidding down slopes of scree – and unflinchingly plunged chest-deep into swift rivers. And she never seemed to tire.

I'd been told by the conservation officer in Kaikoura that Rob, the trek leader, was bringing a group of riders through from Hanmer Springs and they were expected at the Smiths' in the next day or two. Tacker would surely be among them. Alas, the conservation chap had got it wrong. The trek was still several days away.

We talked about Tacker and the trek as we drank tea on the terrace, which overlooked an oasis of garden filled with bright flowers and green foliage that glistened in the sharp afternoon sunlight.

'Do you remember meeting Geoff Parsons last time you were here – he was the older man – my father?' said Nikki.

I'd almost forgotten. Geoff had given me a glimpse of what I was in for on the next eight days of riding. He had spent his life on the other side of the Kaikoura divide, mustering into great flocks the scattered sheep on Bluff Station. 'It's tough country,' he'd said.

'But we were tough men in those days. Out there, there was nothing – no phones, television or radio – just me, my swag and my horse and a menu of dry bread, black billy tea and potatoes. Meat was off the hoof. We were as fit as corn-fed rats,' he'd said wistfully. 'It was a great life. I'd give anything to be out there again.'

I might have agreed with him then, but after the second day of the trek I wasn't so sure. Sitting in the saddle for seven hours, hauling up steep gullies and over precipitous mountain passes in a freezing April fog, lurching down into steep-sided gorges and splashing through icy rivers took its toll. My body felt like stone by the final dismount of the day, cast in the inelegant position that equestrian types might refer to as 'a good seat'. But in another way the second day was also the best, for it was my introduction to the titanic scale and raw beauty of the high country. To be in this type of country was to be immersed in its isolated immensity, to be tired, cold, hungry, stiff and sore – and still be glad to be there, far from the 'featherbed of civilization'.

Over the next few days we crossed the Clarence Reserve and laboured over a rough, misty 1355-metre pass known as Blind Saddle. This had once all been part of the Bluff Station beloved by Geoff. It had been 80,000 hectares in size and carried 60,000 sheep. Now it was split into two: Clarence Reserve and Muzzle Station, to which we were headed. We rested the horses at the Muzzle and stayed in the original Bluff homestead made of cob and iron. The newer version alongside it was home to the current station owners Colin and Tim Nimmo, who were away shopping in Christchurch at the time.

Muzzle was the remotest high-country station left in the South Island. Sipping tea in the sun with the Smiths I felt I was a world away from the day we left the Muzzle, when a gusting nor'wester roared down from the mountain tops, barging through shuddering trees and on into the Clarence River valley. It was followed by solid sheets of rain that blotted out the landscape and ran in rivulets down my neck. I told the Smiths how we'd bent against it, my horse and I, and how I'd battened down my world to her soggy mane and the sweet, thick smell of horse sweat and leather.

'I will never forget arriving in Hanmer Springs eight days, going on eight years, later,' I said, 'with aching bones, a sentimental piece of Tacker's mane and an overwhelming gratitude to be in the vicinity of good food and hot water and the other finer things of life.'

Geoff Parsons was obviously his own man. You'd need to be as tough as old boots to live in that country.

Easy Street

I said goodbye to Claudia and Petra, leaving them outside their tent in the sun sharing a bottle of Steinlager. We drove south through the town and along the coast and then turned inland towards Hanmer Springs, leaving behind an ocean so calm it was as if it had been covered in Glad Wrap. I thought I might have seen a whale blow. The mountains rose majestically to a sharp blue sky broken only by a few wisps of high cloud. It was the first day of spring but even inland, where the weather was warmer, none of the trees had taken much notice. On the sides of the winding road there wasn't a new leaf in sight. But in Hanmer at the motor camp set into the hills behind the town, hints of green had begun to appear on the birches and willow trees.

We could now do our set-up in about twenty minutes. As in every effective partnership there were designated chores. Bill was largely responsible for levelling the caravan and attaching electricity, water and the television. I was in charge of things like untying and re-packing the fridge, unpacking cushions and towels from the cupboards where they'd been stuffed to prevent breakages and spillages, loading the books and spice jars back on their shelves and unloading outdoor items such as the clothes horse and the aerial, chairs and buckets. While the weather was fine we no longer bothered with the awning.

Afterwards I went for a walk beside the river along a track that began at the edge of the camp and then cut a swathe through an extensive pine forest. The mat of pine needles underfoot smelt fresh and rich, and above me a mass of dark trees blotted out the sun. But down by the river the light was blinding and blackberries grew wild. I picked a skirtful and that night boiled them up with sugar to make a small pot of jam.

On the drive to Hanmer Springs Bill and I had added up our funds and decided to forget about working for a while. We'd spend the bit we had accumulated, we decided, and worry about working again when the vault was empty. That was real gypsy thinking – living for the moment. We found ourselves waking up in the morning with nothing on the agenda. And so we wandered through our days, moving from one thing to the next without any sense of purpose. No longer hobbled by the complexities and demands of a modern world, life expanded immeasurably.

Leafing through one of our guidebooks one day, I found a leaf of paper on which was written an old today-list of things to do. It was headed 'Monday 27th'.

Phone calls Peter H, Susan, Jacky, Wine Society, Fernside
Ed meeting 9.30
Meeting with Steven H and Paul, 11 am
Lunch with Diedre, 12.30 Andiamo
Dentist 3.30
Write river story
Talk photography with Megan
Plan for next issue
Check blue books
Update correspondence
Conflict issue…what to do?
Staff presents
Arrange flight to Sydney

Tax???
Car wash
Shoelaces
Dinner?
Deborah and Jim – drinks Friday?

I read it and thought about all the invisibles that used to fill the gaps – what to wear, where to park, how to get there, when to leave, fill up with petrol, water the plants, feed the dog – where the hell are my car keys? I wondered now how I'd stayed sane.

I got up one night in Hanmer Springs and an immense velvet sky dripping with stars was so compelling I found it hard to go back to bed. Next day I stepped into the quiet morning and listened to the sound of bellbirds, and in the freshly unwrapped air I walked with Bill through the waking town. Everybody we passed called out a greeting. We bought bacon and free range eggs and cooked them for brunch. We read and watched the grass grow. I spent time admiring Sammy the hedgehog, who was nosing into a saucer of milk offered by a three-year-old called Jemma.

'I love Thammy,' Jemma told me and she looked at me solemnly with bright amber eyes.

Somewhere inside me a deep contentment began to well, engendered by my enjoyment of these simple occupations. I had found the space that allowed me to register that I was alive, to savour every little thing one by one.

Down at the village I met a man who had perfected the art of living on easy street. In the square a small open-air market was in progress. It was a straggly affair at this quiet time of the year – about fifteen stalls of local crafts and a few well-travelled vegetables. Across the road was parked a large 1948 Ford Jailbar truck that had been converted to a mobile home of weighty proportions. At either end a shingled second storey had been added to form two loft-like living spaces. Everything was painted green except for the window frames, which were a dark tone of mauve.

The owner leant against the side of the truck in the sun. He was dressed in a dark singlet and black jeans, but displayed on every inch of naked skin a twisted mass of tattooed images that, when he moved, took on a life of their own. His head, devoid of hair, was also heavily tattooed and on his chin he wore a tufty beard. Silver rings hung off both ears.

'Just admiring your truck,' I said, not wanting to admit I wanted a closer look at his *art-de-peau*.

A sign on the side of the truck read something like 'Lifeline Tattoo Studio'.

'Er, did you tattoo yourself?' I said, leaning against the front mudguard in a chummy sort of way.

He grinned and shifted position. The artwork danced. 'Some,' he said, 'and friends did the rest.'

'Must have taken a while.'

'Nah, not really. I got my first tattoo when I was fourteen. It was this eagle here.' He pointed to his right forearm. 'Now I reckon about seventy per cent of my body is covered. It's art y'know.'

I nodded.

'Always fascinated me. I'm self-taught. I watched other people doing it and when I thought I knew enough I developed my own designs. Anyway the name's JB. What's yours?'

As he talked JB's fingers moved restlessly against the side of truck as if he itched to pick up the needle. He reached up into the truck and brought down some strange-looking instruments to show me and he pointed out how he sterilised them with a laser. I kept the unsullied canvas of my arms hidden behind my back. JB was one of those self-reliant people who went his own sometimes eccentric way, who wouldn't dream of prying into the affairs of others and didn't expect anyone to meddle in his. But he'd probably be first to help if there was an emergency. He told me he'd been on the road for seventeen years or so.

'Have you ever felt like staying in one place?' I asked.

'Yeah, well it gets a bit tough sometimes. There was one time when I was broke and the truck was crook and wouldn't start. I was in a small place where there was no work and I panicked. I didn't know what the hell I was gonna do. But someone once told me to sit tight in a situation like that because something always happens. And it did. There was a bloke down the road who said he'd fix the engine and I could pay him later, and then I got a bit of a job. A month or so and I was all square and back on the road – no worries. People can be great to you in those sorts of situations. Now I just go along with things and it always turns out okay. We just mooch along and find nice places to park and if we want to we just stay there until something happens or someone moves us on.'

He indicated the woman who'd been standing silently to one side as the other half of the 'we'. A modest tattoo circled her exposed navel, which also had a ring in it. Even though she was young her face told of a bit of living, but when she smiled the warmth went all the way to her hazel eyes. Her auburn hair was caught up behind her head in a scrappy pile and on every digit of each hand was a silver ring.

'It's a good life,' she offered. 'We can go where we want. Everywhere is home to us. I've been with JB for two years now and I love it.' She told me she made window hangings out of crystals and wire curls and sold them in the markets.

'The markets are the best places to earn a living,' said JB. 'But you can't just pitch up in town and set up. You have to have a hawker's licence and set up a certain distance from any competing business. Each town has its own rules.'

'If I offered you, say, half a million dollars, do you think you'd change your lifestyle?' I said.

He shot me a look that was incredulous yet hopeful, like a dog who'd been offered a piece of scotch fillet off the table. He thought about it. 'Nah,' he said finally. 'I'd have gone on the road whatever and I'll always be on it. I'd just buy a few bigger toys. Maybe I'd go to Aussie for a bit.'

He asked me where I was staying.

'In the park down the road. We live in a caravan,' I said.

'Oh yeah, how much does that cost you?'

'About a hundred and twenty dollars a week.'

'All up?'

'No, just the rent.'

'Wow,' he said. 'That's all we need to live on in a good week. We'd buy our tucker, our diesel and a few beers for that. We eat well – plenty of vegies and big roasts in the winter.' He licked his lips at the thought of it.

In a world grown exhaustingly complex, JB's back-to-basics grip on life seemed as tempting as home-baked scones.

A couple of days later, when we left Hanmer Springs, JB was also clearing out. The Safari with caravan in tow ground past him as his great Jailbar lumbered with weighty dignity through the town. We exchanged big-arm waves out our open windows. I felt a sense of belonging. We too could go wherever we wanted.

Boutique Lodgings

Several weeks later we were ambling around Oamaru conjuring up images of Janet Frame's early life when Leanne Holdsworth rang my cellphone. She and her husband published a book called *Boutique Lodgings of New Zealand*, a directory of cottages, lodges and B&Bs throughout the country. I'd only met Leanne once and I didn't think she would remember me.

'I heard through the grapevine that you and Bill were on the road,' she said, 'and we really need someone to do the reviews of the properties that are already in the book, and any new ones, for the fourth edition. Do you think the two of you would be interested? It means you will be on the road for several months but the pay is good.'

It sounded like a project with potential and so I flew to Auckland to talk it over. Leanne collected me at the airport and drove me to the same coffee bar in Ponsonby where before we started on our journey my friend had asked me, in so many words, what the hell I thought I was doing. In my new state of being Auckland seemed frantic, overstuffed and wildly out of control.

When we had talked business and finished two cups of coffee, Leanne dropped me off at my old offices in Hargreaves Street. I went first to find my colleagues in administration on the fourth floor. As I stood at the reception desk expecting to be welcomed as someone of some importance, I had a sharp lesson in the transitory nature of prestige. A young employee, looking primped – rather priggish actually – rushed up to me. 'Oh goodie,' she said, 'are you the sandwich lady?'

I hailed a taxi to take me back to the airport. It was driven by a Polynesian man of about fifty who had short cropped hair, a cheery smile and a neck that bulged above his collar. His breathing was noisy – the laboured wheeze of the overfed. Sitting in the back of his impeccably kept white Toyota Corona I noticed that whenever he could take his eyes off the road he was glancing at me in the rear-vision mirror. Then my eyes met his.

'Are you saved?' he said.

'Excuse me?'

'Are you saved?'

'Saved from what exactly?'

It was all he needed to launch into the most astonishing onslaught. 'From the depths of hell,' he said, his voice rising. 'From the wages of sin, from the evil that invades your soul, from fornication with the devil.' He wagged a finger skyward as if he were conducting a piece of music. 'For the Lord said, "As ye sow, so shall ye reap." You must be saved by the love of God through the power of prayer or eternal damnation will be yours.'

His voice began to boom. My driver was no longer behind the wheel; he was in his pulpit. 'I can pray for you, my sister,' he thundered. 'I am a preacher. I have saved many many many through the power of prayer, through the love of our Lord who saves only those who turn to him. I can save your soul for Christ.'

'Yes, yes,' I said. Then, 'Of course, of course.' Then, 'Absolutely.' And I started to pray – that he would not go off the road and that I would arrive unscathed and unsaved at the airport terminal.

As I was handing him his fare the taxi-preacher-man said in a moderated tone, 'Thank you ma'am. We must all do what we've come here to do, you know.'

I was completely floored. I'd come to Auckland to look at a line of work and I took his words as an omen. A week or so later Bill and I signed the contract and found ourselves charged with visiting over 200 lodges, cottages and B&Bs around the country, collecting gradings, writing text and taking photographs. This gave our wandering more structure but it was one way of keeping solvent on the way.

Over the next six months we covered the country from North Cape to Bluff. Things in the accommodation industry had been lively in the previous few seasons. Tourists had flocked to New Zealand and their presence had helped to feather some very swanky nests throughout the country. Cottages, houses and farm buildings had been converted, renovated and constructed to cater for the influx. Some grand old historic homes had been saved from dereliction – Fernside in the Wairarapa, Corstorphine House and Lisburn House in Dunedin, Tighnafeile House in Timaru, The Weston House and Hadleigh Heritage Home in Christchurch were just a few that had been refurbished, polished and preened to near perfection.

Most were run by people who had never been in the hospitality industry before. By the time we'd researched all the material for the book I had developed a great admiration for the inventiveness, creativity, enterprise and sheer hard graft with which many of these hosts ran their businesses.

To me it didn't look like much fun to organise canapes and drinks, then cook an inspired three-course dinner with everything just so, and then sit around being cheerful and entertaining until your guests (who were on holiday) decided to drink one more liqueur before they dragged themselves off to bed. Then to clean up their mess and yours before you staggered off to bed yourself. Then to get up at sparrow fart the next morning in order to present your guests, as they arrived in stages according to their whim, with a gourmet breakfast over which they could linger until about eleven o'clock. And when they had departed for the next stage of their journey, wash and iron four pairs of king-sized sheets and twenty-four pillowcases and six towels, clean each bathroom so there was not a single pubic hair in sight and each bedroom so there was not a grain of dust, before the next guests arrived at three in the afternoon.

To do this day after day without rest would be enough to drive most people up the bedroom wall, out the window and off to another life. Many of the hosts we encountered didn't just bend over backwards to ensure their guests had a good time, they turned somersaults. That they entertained from the heart, gave service without servitude, and did it with such good humour and generosity of spirit was, to me, nothing short of remarkable.

Sometimes we stayed in the lodges or B&Bs but often we kept to the caravan. It might seem too good to be true to earn one's living dashing about the country staying in beautifully appointed accommodation and having breakfast and dinner prepared for you every day. It was. We would have lost our reason after a while if we hadn't been able to step back into our own space where we could be slippered and silent, where we could shovel corned beef and cabbage into our mouths and pick our teeth while we watched *Coronation Street*.

Once we took a break to do some house-sitting. Over Christmas Judy and Peter Rann were off to France and we agreed to abandon the caravan and look after their Albany house, their large section, their boxer dog called Chelsea and half a dozen chooks. The house opened onto a large terrace that overlooked fruit trees, a swimming pool, sweeping lawns and bush beyond. The Ranns' hens were caged and well behaved, reliably laying an egg each every day in the provided straw.

From next door, however, a foraging party of four brown shavers brazenly trespassed on our lawn on a daily basis and they didn't lay anything on our side of the fence. I gave them names. There was Star, who held her head high and minced across the grass as if she was on a catwalk, Scoffer who examined everything as if it might turn out to be something good to eat, Penny who kept cocking an eye heavenward as if waiting for the sky to fall in, and poor Henrietta who kept flattening herself against the ground, as if she expected to be the victim of some form of violence.

I took the opportunity to gather friends at the long wooden table on the deck for lunches of pasta and salads and decorative breads with olive oil so that we could pretend (seeing everyone seemed to be off to Europe those days) that we were somewhere in the Mediterranean.

At the first such gathering my daughter Inge, who had always had a sharp eye, spotted something glittering in the grass. It was a piece of tinfoil that led her to a bush, behind which she discovered a bright trail of ripped-up cardboard.

'My Christmas presents!' she wailed, and raced inside to look under the Christmas tree.

The three boxes of chocolates she had wrapped that morning were intact, but my two large, double-layered, rather expensive chocolates, also wrapped and left in a basket in the bedroom, had disappeared. By a singular coincidence, so had Chelsea. Her guilt was unavoidable. She was shitting little bits of tinfoil for the next three days.

My second lunch was a dashing affair. Several well-attired women wearing linen shirts and Gucci sunglasses, with antique gold chains around their necks and wide-brimmed straw hats perched on their heads, were lingering on the deck sipping their second or third glass of Sauvignon Blanc and nibbling the cheeses. Chelsea arrived, wagging her rump and tail-stump with glee and carrying in her mouth what appeared to be a feather duster. Then she presented at my feet the headless body, oozing blood and entrails, of Star. The well-attired women set up a squeaking chorus of ooohs and aaahs and fled indoors.

Sadly, over the next week Scoffer, Henrietta and Penny all went to the great nesting box in the sky in the same manner. Not one of them had the sense to stay on their own side of the fence. I could have told them that it wasn't always a wise thing to go looking for greener pastures.

Wild Romancing

By the time we had finished work on the book, the parts of the country Bill and I felt we could call home were starting to expand. More and more places were feeling like our own backyard, places where we had friends who made us welcome and local knowledge that made us insiders – handy snippets like where to find the butcher with the best sausages, the bread shop that baked crunchy-crusted loaves, the best place to take shoes to be mended or the Postshop where there was a jar of free jelly beans on the counter.

Possibly as a result of this familiarity, or perhaps because every day was different, I was totally free of yearnings. Every morning I woke up in a place I was happy to be in – even if it was being buffeted by a wind straight from the Antarctic at Riverton, or crowded into the show grounds at Invercargill with twenty-five canine lovers and a couple of hundred dogs at the annual dog show. There were, of course, places that went straight to the heart. One of those would be the Catlins. But before we went there I begged to spend a week in Dunedin.

The Catlins was to be a new experience, but Dunedin was as familiar as an old pair of socks. Impressions, memories and experiences were layered and intertwined. The past gave texture to the present and for me Dunedin had a texture as thick as a tartan blanket. My Scottish forebears went there fleeing the Highland Clearances and looking for safety in a land that resembled their own. Almost a hundred years later I arrived in Dunedin to do my training at the physiotherapy school. And those tangled times – of grappling with the enormities of sex and exams and fear of pregnancy, of poverty, of relationships, of studying in the freezing cold in a big brick house in Elder Street, drinking beer at the Bowling Green and cappuccinos at Checkers Restaurant, waitressing at the Savoy Hotel, and getting drunk on apple cider – could not be divorced from my experience of the city now.

I walked past the old med school where in the 'bod room' we had dissected self-gifted bodies pickled in something like formaldehyde. Mine was that of a slim old woman with white hair, which had a pink bow still neatly tied to a strand of it. I had called her Lily.

I found again the small cottage in the Leith valley where four medical students of my acquaintance were, rumour had it, faced with a body in rather different circumstances. A distressed middle-aged neighbour had woken them in the night and announced that her lover, who was married to someone else, appeared to be dead in her bed. He had, the students ascertained, almost certainly died from a heart attack. The story went that they dressed the unfortunate man and carried his earthly remains to the nearest park bench, where they arranged them comfortably and where they were discovered in the morning. The man's reputation was intact and his wife, who had to suffer her husband's death, was spared the double whammy that he was also a philanderer.

Laid over these bizarre sorts of memories were my new impressions of Dunedin – the dignity I'd never noticed before in its hills clustered with houses, in the huge, sombre stone buildings that spoke of its prosperous past and in the marvellously ornate railway station. And I added to these memories the wandering albatrosses of the peninsula, conversations with Isaac who lived in a boathouse at Port Chalmers, damp cool walks through the trees of the green belt, and pasta and chicken with Olivia who told me she had dressed up as Scarlett O'Hara for her wedding. My Dunedin was a jumble of nostalgia for my youth, pangs of sadness for the way things had not been as I expected, and delight in what I found in the city as it was today.

We had three choices about how to spend our time at Easter: we could stay put, travel north to the Mackenzie Highland Show with its promise of cooking, bottling, needlework, piping, highland dancing, wood chopping, lolly scrambles, pet lamb parade and dog trials, or we could follow the love train to Middlemarch.

Middlemarch won. We were lured to that tiny town, 77 kilometres from Dunedin at the foot of the Rock and Pillar Range, by its ecstatic preparation for the impending invasion of love seekers to the singles dance. The town's population of a hundred or so was expected to treble for the weekend. For only the third time in its twelve-year history, the Orchard Sun Club had received bookings for its accommodation; Blind Billy's campsite was almost full. Preparations for the big weekend were being carefully juggled with harvesting, drenching, tupping and feeding.

The talk might have been of romance but roses, champagne, soft music and candle-lit dinners were not part of the plan. Preparations were of a more pragmatic nature – the store and service station ordered condoms by the boxful, the pub organised a licence to stay open all weekend and a special delivery of Speight's, and the Pog 'n' Scroggin Bush Band was brought in to provide the music.

We set off for the village on Sunday, the day after the Midnight Express had departed from Dunedin and already returned with its load of love-lucky or lovelorn party-goers who had attended the singles dance. By the time we rode into town there was little sign of the revelry except for a large marquee. I wandered inside expecting to see a writhing couple or two, or at least one abandoned condom, but all that remained were a drum and a lonely blue balloon trailing a string and floating near the ceiling.

Everyone I asked said, without elaborating, that the night had been a great success. Everyone that is except for the man in the pub where Bill and I went for a midday beer after our long hot drive across the Strath Taieri plateau. We ordered two cans of Speight's, no glasses thanks. I occupied myself by looking around. A large Captain Cooker pig's head graced one wall and a notice on the door to the dining room said 'No boots allowed'. There were macho advertisements for beer everywhere, depicting toughened men, horses and wagons braving mountain terrain and torrential rivers. One had a caption that read 'Drink Draught with a Mate'. Another informed me that a Southern Man admired a woman who could drink a handle of Speight's and never sat down at the bar.

There were a television, a poker machine and on one wall a picture of a large digger bogged in a deep ditch. The notice underneath it read, 'New digger driver required'. I was peering at this when a young man in a red Swanndri, perched groggily on a stool at the bar just behind me, leant over and said, 'Reckon you could do the job?' He laughed heartily at his own joke.

I smiled wanly and asked him if by any chance he'd been to the dance the night before.

'Yep, I went but I had too much piss to get lucky. Anyway sheilas from the city aren't too interested in us tussocks. They know it means working on a farm and isolation and that, and they don't go for it.'

'Perhaps you could move somewhere else. You might have more luck.'

'Nah, I don't reckon. Me mates are here.'

I pointed to a trickle of congealed blood running from his temple hairline to his chin.

'What happened to you?'

'Got into a bit of a scrap.' He grinned lopsidedly. 'Nothin' serious.'

On the way out of town we called in to the horse show. Almost the first person I saw as we came through the gate was Brenda astride a little chestnut mare. Brenda was one of those women whose age would never keep her out of the saddle – even though, as she confided, her hips were letting her down a bit.

'I could need a crane soon to get me on and off the blinking thing,' she said.

Anyone in Otago who owned a horse, or aspired to, probably knew Brenda. She was a woman with a no-nonsense-just-get-on-with-it approach to life and a very generous spirit. Three years earlier I had got to know her well when she lent me a thoroughbred mare called Rosie to ride in the seven-day Cavalcade, an annual event that followed the gold trails of Central Otago. Brenda had done the trip in a pony trap and I admired her immensely for it. It took a bit of guts – she wasn't a young woman and the country we travelled through wasn't easy.

I was thrilled to see her again. She invited Bill and me back to the horsebox, where we drank weak tea out of yellow mugs and sat on the floor among the horse shit and hay and relived the highlights of the ride.

'You've got to come on the next one,' she said. 'Give us a ring and I'll get a horse for you. And any time you're in Dunedin you two've got to drop in. Door's always open. If we're not there, just grab a bed. We won't be more than a couple o' days away. What you see is what you get, but you're always welcome.'

I said yes to both suggestions and hoped that we'd be able to take her up on them.

Back in Dunedin we ate dinner and packed up the caravan ready for an early start. The camp was cold and soggy and full of wet children trying to make the most of their Easter break by playing shrieking games around the ablution block. We weren't sorry to leave.

The next day was fine, just a smear or two of cloud and the breeze rhythmically moving the treetops. On our way south we turned off the main route at Lake Waihola and followed a narrow, winding dirt road for about 20 kilometres to the mouth of the Taieri River. Alan (married to Scarlett O'Hara), the chef of a reputable restaurant in Dunedin, had told us that there we could buy the freshest fish in the South Island.

On the south bank of the river we discovered the little booth where Heather and Keith ran their business. There were only a handful of fishing people in the country who had a licence to sell straight from their own boat, and they were among them. Behind the counter was Heather, a prosaic, cheery woman who was happy to pass the time of day as she picked out the blue cod, brill and sole and slapped it between white paper for her customers.

'We've been here twenty-five years,' she grinned. 'Keith was an electrician before we came here and started fishing. We never meant to stay that long, but we can't imagine where we would go from here.'

'Buy a caravan,' I said, 'and you can go anywhere you like.'

'I suppose we could always tow the boat,' she grinned.

Her husband, his face half hidden by a sou'wester, was on board the *Nikita*, their ship-shape fishing launch tied to the jetty just behind the booth. He was filleting blue cod with the sure-handed, rhythmical action of long practice. He took a cod from the bucket, dipped it in a trough, laid it on a stainless-steel bench, slid the knife down one side, flipped the fish, slid the knife down the other, carefully laid the gleaming fillets on top of the growing pile and threw the carcass into a bucket. Each fish took twenty seconds.

That night we lightly pan-fried a feast of this delicious flesh, which needed nothing more than a squeeze of lemon to make it memorable. We were camped at Balclutha, a small service town that had cleaved to the banks of the Clutha for the last century or so, despite the river's best attempts to sweep it away. The only feature of any note was a graceful concrete bridge with bow-shaped arches spanning the wide and murky river that muttered past the town.

Next day we left the caravan behind and drove a few kilometres south of Balclutha, where a left turn led to the coast and Nugget Point – a spectacle well worth a dusty drive. This high ridge with a lighthouse on its pinnacle poked out into the Pacific Ocean. Beyond it a collection of sea stacks were scattered like knucklebones in the water, each surrounded by a swirling skirt of bull kelp.

The Nuggets were home to a fascinating array of coastal wildlife. We walked towards the lighthouse along the narrow ridge above the sea. Even from this height I could hear the eerie, echoing bark of seals and catch a whiff of their pungent presence among the rocky outcrops below. And there they were, crowded into rocky pools, splashing and dashing about like gaggles of children at the municipal baths. On the other side of the ridge Hooker's sea lions snoozed among carpets of drying kelp. At that distance they looked like giant garden slugs until something irritated them; then they moved with lightning speed. This was a marvellous place. Out on the sea spotted shags and sooty shearwaters rested – vast flotillas of them sprinkled over the water's surface like hundreds and thousands. Gannets nested there, as did little blue penguins, yellow-eyed penguins and lately royal spoonbills. Rockhopper penguins stopped over to moult and three types of crested penguins visited from time to time, although there were none when we were there.

The sight of all this wildlife thrilled me. Time in Africa had given me a profound respect for all forms of life and an insight into how tightly woven together they were. This had filled me with a zeal to see them preserved. But I'd more recently come to accept that in a money-driven world fish, forests, birds and animals had to earn the right to exist. And so to see these sea creatures clustered around Nugget Point and people clustered on the ridge above to look down and enjoy them was a triumph of sorts. They'd be safe as long as people came to enjoy them.

Galloping Sea Lions

The tiny town of Owaka had eftpos and cappuccino, but it would be the last of such modern amenities before Bluff. Owaka marked the beginning of the Catlins Coastal Rainforest Park, which took up a large chunk of the south-eastern corner of the island. It was characterised by a chain of bush reserves of rimu, southern rata and kamahi, a coast of steep and craggy headlands, reedy estuaries and a great crescent sweep of sea-battered golden sand. I hope that, in writing about my love of the area's rugged good looks, of the pockets of forests that cascade down the hills to blend into the sand dunes and its laid-back unself-conscious lifestyle, I don't destroy the very things I keep going back for.

We spent a week at the campsite by the estuary at Pounawea, not far from where the Catlins and Owaka Rivers bled into the sea. The campsite was small, surrounded by totara and pepper trees, and the amenities were basic but scrubbed clean. The only other people in the camp were fishermen and families from Invercargill who had brought their tents and caravans north for the weekend. At night when the tide was out the kids collected together and went fishing for flounder with home-made spears or hunting for crabs by torchlight. Their shouts stirred in me long-buried memories of an estuary in Hawke's Bay, and my sister flailing a pointed stick in the air like a lunatic warrior, on the night she had stood by mistake on the flounder she was meant to be spearing.

Every morning we were woken by a chorus of tui that, with their ringing melodies, claimed the area as their own. The birds in the Catlins were more numerous than in other parts of the country, where stoats and rats and possums had all but silenced the bush. As we were walking down the road one evening Bill was suddenly brought to a halt. 'Look at that,' he yelled, and up from the trees there rose in unison about seventy kereru. We had never seen so many native pigeons all at once.

A fellow camper told me that up the Catlins River there was a small colony of yellowheads that could with patience sometimes be seen. Yellowheads were rare – just a few pockets of them were left around the country. To a birdwatcher like me, of course, the less common the bird the greater its allure.

Bill found himself a handy nine-hole golf course near Pounawea and one day, after he went off with his clubs looking pleased and purposeful, I packed a lunch and drove to the store in Owaka to find a map and directions for the river. An old, frayed-looking man in a dusty suit was sitting in the sun outside the pub. He told me he'd hunted for gold up around there a long time earlier.

'Never found a thing,' he said.

I asked him what he would have done with the money if he'd struck it rich.

'Oh, it was never the money, lass,' he said. 'I just wanted gold to hold in my hand.'

He instructed me on how to find the track that led to the river by waving his arms in wide circles to indicate direction, confusing me totally and then summarising his efforts by saying, 'You can't miss it,' which meant I probably would.

But this time I found the road more-or-less straight away and coaxed the Safari along it, at first past farmland, then by the river and then winding higher and higher through the forest as the river fell away in the gully below. About an hour off the main road I found a path leading down through the forest on my left. I parked the vehicle as close to the edge of the road as I dared, so that if perchance any other vehicle came this way it could squeeze past and I wouldn't have an irate driver fuming around my truck kicking in the side panels when I came back. I didn't think there was much to worry about. It didn't look as if a car had been that way for months.

I felt alone and rather vulnerable when I started out along the track. It was beautiful but uncannily still, as if something momentous was about to happen. There was a hovering reverence as if the lofty silver beeches were at prayer. At ground level, ferns sprouted thickly and light that filtered through the tiny leaves above bounced against the mosses and wove patterns on the carpet of dead leaves. I became intoxicated by the scent of warm earth and damp foliage, and as I listened to my own footfalls I began to feel as if the forest were absorbing me. I had a place like this in my mind, an inner sanctuary I could retreat to when I needed reassurance; and so in the solitude of the forest I started to feel not just at peace, but as if I had come home.

And then from up in the canopy came a faint *tssst tsst* and a tiny shadow flitted past me like a spirit. It came again, teasing me, vanishing before I could grasp that it was there. I leant against an old tree encrusted with pale green lichen and raised my binoculars to the tops. There it was. Its brilliant yellow head gave it away as it busily searched for food, dashing from branch to branch and thoroughly inspecting each leaf and twig from all angles and prying nosily into all the little cracks and crevices. It allowed me a glimpse that possibly only lasted a minute but gave me the sort of satisfaction that only a fellow birdwatcher would understand. I returned to the camp feeling immensely pleased with my day.

Bill turned sixty in the Catlins. The milestone passed without much fanfare, I'm afraid. We cooked some rather suspect steak on the barbecue and drank a bottle of cheap champagne. We wove through the bush down to the estuary to look at the stars swimming in the inky sky and listen to the waves slapping against the shore, and then we went to bed. I would have liked to have given Bill the sight of that yellowhead for his birthday but he assured me that a packet of golf balls…perhaps a trip to Alaska…would suit him just as well.

W e could have spent a year wandering the bush walks and the estuaries and the tiny communities that dotted the landscape of the Catlins, and examining the oddities that made up the nature of the place. One was the tumultuously spectacular Jacks Blowhole. It was named after Bloody Jack, as he was dubbed by the whalers. He was actually Hone Tuhawaiki, paramount chief of Ngai Tahu. I never discovered if the blowhole was named after him because he discovered it, owned it or jumped into it in a fit of depression.

One cold blustery day we drove to the unprepossessing Slope Point, a place that formed the southernmost tip of the South Island. The land here sloped down to the sea, which I supposed was how the point got its name. But slopier still were the stands of macrocarpa trees, shaped like wind-blown hair by the force of the gales racing up from the Antarctic. I would like to be able to report that I thought a profound thought or two, for if there was a place called the End of the Earth this could have been it. In reality it was too cold to think of anything except getting out of the wind.

Just around the corner from Slope Point was a real Jurassic Park called Curio Bay. It was famous because embedded in its rocky tidal platform was an array of fossilised tree trunks dating back to the middle Jurassic age (about 160 million years ago). This was a figure I found hard to relate to; very, very old had to do. Around the edge of the bay the sea bashed in a fearsome way against the rocks, and in deep and hellish pits and crevasses great forests of kelp swirled and gyrated like giant sea snakes. I watched with fascinated horror and imagined what would happen to me if I fell in. A yellow-eyed penguin, its feet bright pink from the cold, cruised in on a wave and landed on a patch of sand. It shook itself a few times and waddled up the beach to its burrow like a little fat gnome with arthritic knees.

Adjacent to Curio Bay was Porpoise Bay. Not far out from the rocks there we saw three Hector's dolphins arching out of the sea in unison. Their silver flanks glistened for a second above the surface and then they disappeared into the churning waves. These little sea creatures were so rare it was good just to know they were there.

We had our biggest wildlife thrill at Surat Bay one evening where on the beach, just a few metres away, a group of young male Hooker's sea lions had hauled out on the shortbread-coloured sand. They were black and blubbery with great thrusting chests and enormous pink-lined mouths that they frequently opened wide as if inviting us to inspect their tonsils. The females, I had read, were small, sandy coloured and quite cute, but there was nothing cute about these chaps. They roared like bulls and, despite their enormous weight, could move at impressive speeds.

They let us come quite close but the only other person on the beach, a German man with long legs and a long camera lens, took liberties. I will never forget the less-than-graceful sight of a German in shorts and roman sandals sprinting across the beach yelling, 'Nein! Nein!' while being pursued by 400 kilograms of galloping sea lion that a moment earlier had been snoozing benignly by the water flicking sand over his back with his flippers. I don't think the German will ever forget it either.

There were lots of watery places to walk to in the Catlins – wild beaches, gaping estuaries ribbed with muddy sand at low tide, salt marshes, river mouths clogged with jointed reeds, waterfalls, lakes and stony streams purling down from the hills. There was a dark puddle of black reflective water that was the 'hanging' lake named Wilkie, and a pitiful little dribble of water about a metre high some wit had called Niagara Falls.

Tied to the bank of the sluggish Owaka River estuary was an old scow almost hidden by a clump of trees. The scow looked forlorn and uncared for and every day I passed it I became increasingly curious. Eventually I asked the woman at the cramped little camp office at Pounawea what the story was. 'Oh, that's the Portland,' she said. 'It belongs to a fella called Ray from the West Coast. I dunno what he's doing with it. It's been there for years. As far back as I can remember.'

'Does Ray live around here?'

'I dunno where he lives. Maybe on the boat sometimes.'

The day before we left Pounawea on our way to Papatowai I noticed someone sitting on a plank about half way down the bow of the *Portland*. The plank was fixed like a swing with a rope at each end. The man, dressed in grey overalls, was slapping bright blue paint onto the old girl's sides with an enormous brush.

I crashed through the trees and yelled, 'Hello there,' in what I thought was a chummy nautical tone.

No response.

'Umm excuse me.'

The man slowly put down his brush, pushed the lid carefully onto his tin of paint and turned his head. 'Yeah gidday.'

'I'm just being nosy really. Can you tell me when she was built?' I said, trying to sound as if I knew a thing or two about boats.

'Dunno. Better ask the owner.' He pointed to the bank and I turned to see a tall bulky man standing watching me from the shadow of a small shed tucked under the trees.

'You must be Ray.'

'Yep, you'd be right,' he said.

Ray was not dressed for company. His hands were blackened with dirt, his khaki shirt and trousers streaked with grease and goodness knew what else. He looked suspiciously at the notebook in my hand. 'You one of those journalists?' he said.

I was a writer and there *was* a difference. 'Nah,' I said, hoping I sounded convincing.

Ray warmed up bit by bit when he saw I was genuinely interested. He told me the *Portland* was built of four-inch-thick kauri in 1910. She was the only surviving hold scow in the country, which was not all that surprising because only seventeen were ever built. In the 1930s she was based in Nelson and carried apples and timber from Golden Bay and Motueka to Wellington. She crossed Cook Strait over 10,000 times.

'Seeing you're interested,' said Ray, 'I'll show you over. But we don't usually have women around. She's pretty rough.'

He wasn't wrong. The hold had been reroofed and Ray and the painter, whose name was Arthur, had made a snug for themselves inside. They'd installed a wood-fired range to cook on and erected a rough bench on which two enamel mugs and jars of sugar and coffee rested, and they had a very old fridge. Up forward were a couple of bunks with thin mattresses that might have been made of straw, piled with grey blankets. An old bench seat covered in stained vinyl served as the lounge suite. No prizes for decor but, as Ray said, it was a bachelor pad. I declined to view the toilet and bathroom.

'When we get things tidied up a bit she'll be great,' said Ray. 'I've had her for twenty-one years.'

'Have you sailed in her in that time?'

'Not much. I just like owning her. You know, like some people own a Rembrandt. The difference is that I'm seventy-one and she's ninety-one and needs a lot of looking after.'

Ray's plan was to take her to Greymouth via the Marlborough Sounds that year and put her in the slips. I'd place a bet that she is still tied up in the estuary today. After so long, she's probably glued to the bottom.

Whisky Galore

It wasn't clear how we ended up in Gore – it wasn't a place that held much appeal. And when we did arrive there it was locked in a frosty mantle of fog that did nothing to dispel that notion. But in the end I liked Gore much more than I had expected to. It had two great claims to fame: whisky and oatmeal porridge, so it was not hard to work out that the roots of the place were Scottish. The Southland burr could be quite pronounced there: 'Och, it's foin in Gorrre.' Although that could be overdoing it.

It wasn't the burr that the highlanders wanted to keep when they arrived. What they wanted more than anything was to hang on to their spirit – in the form of 'highland dew'. Bill and I called in to the Howling at the Moon bar, a reasonably modern looking place on the main street, and ordered a whisky each. We did this for three reasons: to warm our cockles with the demon drink, to warm our toes in front of a robust fire, and just because we could.

After 1902 not a drop of grog was legally consumed in Gore for the next fifty-five years. The Temperance Society, prohibitionists and wowsers were a formidable force there, but equally determined were the brewers, distillers and distributors. The town and district were declared dry, which meant there was probably more grog drunk there than ever before. Home brewers and distillers were never seen but they were everywhere – in the Hokonui hills, and in the backyards, cellars, garages and probably the back bedrooms of the town.

The term sly grogging originated in Gore and so did the ritual of keg parties, when beer was brought in from outside the district. It sounded like the Wild West, with the town divided into those who did and those who didn't, and a network of informers, police and profiteers playing one side off against the other.

I examined a photograph taken in the 1920s, which I came across in the Hokonui Moonshine Museum. It showed a row of about twenty taxis lined up along the road. Sue, who was the curator of the museum and something of a historian, told me that it would have been taken at five o'clock, knock-off time, when the taxis waited in Gore's main street to whiz workers to Mandeville and the nearest wet pub, more than 20 kilometres away. 'Pubs closed at six in those days,' she said, 'and it took them twenty minutes to get there. But they still managed to get a skinful in the time that was left.'

We were in Gore on Anzac Day and we had another whisky at the local RSA, where the grogging was anything but sly. There was a hearty singsong going on in one corner, where a voluptuous vocalist in a black satin outfit was crooning a Country and Western version of 'Underneath the Lamplight' – with some success. I studied the photographs of local men who had gone to the wars, many of whom never came home. They were as young as my son, with smooth skins and proud postures. Their expressions were solemn but there was no hint of fear or horror. Not yet. No one took photographs of them if they returned.

As I stood there in front of the gallery a fortyish man, his hair sticky with gel and a gold filling in one tooth of a set that was too white to be his own, came tipsily towards me. He took an extravagant gulp of his whisky and, swaying slightly, stuck out a meaty hand. 'You'rrre welcome,' he said, smiling so broadly I thought his teeth might fall out. 'Lookin' at our boys are you? It was all a bad thing, terrible terrible thing.' His face fell and then brightened in the exaggerated way that drunks tend to express themselves. 'You're very very welcome here. You have a very good time now.' He left abruptly, leaving me smiling and nodding to the wall.

I found the most poignant expression of Anzac Day at the town's large cenotaph, an imposing obelisk surrounded by gardens, tennis courts and croquet lawns. Among the wreaths of poppies and roses was one with a card that read, 'In loving remembrance of my loving brothers, Sgt George A Jones, missing North Sea, Scotland, 1942. Pvt Sydney B Jones, missing Crete, May 1941, 1st Echelon. Pvt Alan R Jones, 3rd Echelon, Egypt. Alexander H Jones, NZ Air Force in the islands. Gordon D Jones, NZ Air Force in the islands. Your loving sister Mabel.' I thought beyond the words to their mother's pain. I struggled with the thought of living the rest of my life without one of my daughters. How could any mother survive the loss of two sons, knowing that three more were in active service?

Gore's other claim to fame (apart from a Roman Catholic church that looked like a UFO and the annual Gold Guitar country music awards) had a more cheerful connection with the armed forces in the chubby figure of Sergeant Dan. The large logo of this angelic boy in a scout's uniform with a toy rifle over his shoulder was painted on the side of the Fleming's Oatmeal Mill building in the centre of town. Any New Zealander of a certain age and worth his or her porridge had for breakfast at some stage of their lives a bowl of Creamoata and cream – and maybe brown sugar.

I could still hear my grandmother's singsong voice reciting as she ladled out porridge in the morning:

Says Sergeant Dan, recruitment man:
We're bound to get our quota

If youngsters all obey the call
And train upon Creamoata.

This ditty came from an advertisement for Creamoata in a Red Cross recipe book published in 1916.

Oat milling had been carried out in Gore for nearly a hundred years but at about the time we arrived in the town the operation ceased, not because it had become unprofitable but because it was more profitable for its principals to sell the Gore mill and confine manufacture to Australia. An aggrieved local had climbed up the wall of the Fleming's building and painted a large tear on Sergeant Dan's cheek.

We drove out of Gore, past the treeless Hokonui hills glowing in the afternoon sunshine. More-or-less on the spur of the moment, we had decided to go to Central Otago before the winter of our second year on the road got a grip. In my years of visiting the place I'd never grown blasé about the way the mountains, towns, sunlight, snow and waterscapes in Central existed in such spectacular harmony. The ungraspable scale of the landscape and the intensity of the elements always stirred in me feelings of both awe and dread. And there was no way of quite capturing the memory of those stark and arid heights, the raw rockiness of the bizarre canyons or the scale of the bony ranges that crashed into each other like herds of gargantuan elephants.

Our first stop was in Arrowtown. We parked at the camp, which was also the local football field. We were the only campers there. There was nothing flash about the facilities but the surroundings were stunning. I put on my warmest jacket and sat outside to watch the sun setting. It lit the rocky tops of the hills so that they glowed like the embers of a coal fire. Then a full moon rose into the night sky like a huge snowball before a heavy fog came down, fuzzing out the street lamps and muffling the sounds from the village.

In the early morning the fog lifted like a theatre curtain, revealing bit by bit the hills behind the town, which were aflame with autumn leaves turned ruby, orange, umber, saffron and ochre. The air was fresh, with a slightly earthy odour. Bill and I stoked our lungs by walking to the village, wading along the way through a thick carpet of wet leaves and jumping around to catch ones that were falling like flirtatious fairies as they made their final journey to the ground. I felt sixteen again.

But I had work to do. Someone had phoned me from an Auckland magazine to write about some of the lodges we'd visited. 'There's very little time,' she'd said. 'Frankly we're in a bit of a panic. Would four days be enough?' I had to ignore the wonderful environment outside and turn myself over to earning some money.

When I had a good work station surrounded by all my reference books and the other paraphernalia that writing required, it wasn't too hard to turn words out at speed, but in the small space of a caravan it could be like wading through glue. I had to haul out everything I needed from the cupboard under the squabs, unpack it and set it up every time I wanted to use it. If we needed to use the table for something else, I had to put it all away again. And I seemed to spend my life on my knees, ferreting around on the floor among books and bits of paper for some reference or other.

Two days later the woman from the magazine rang again. 'Oh, could you please send a photograph of yourself for the contributors' page. We need it by tomorrow or the next day if possible.'

I spent maybe an hour tarting myself up, then Bill lined me up against on old shed and shot a roll of film. I grabbed it and drove the half hour to Queenstown, getting there just in time to snatch a courier bag from the Postshop and get the film to a camera shop. I waited for two hours while it was developed. The images weren't great – a year on the road had done little for my appearance – but I knew they'd have to do. It was now six-thirty at night.

Next morning back in Arrowtown I jumped out of bed and

jogged down the road to post the film by the required time of nine o'clock. At ten o'clock the woman from the magazine rang again.

'Oh, and could you please send a brief bio,' she asked in a tone that implied she was doing me an immense favour.

I changed my plans for the day, raced back to the caravan and knocked out 200 words that I then couldn't email because something had gone awry with my technological wizardry. It was about three o'clock in the afternoon before the bio went racing off through the ether to meet the deadline.

Two days later, another phone call. 'Where are the photos?' she bleated.

'I've no idea. I couriered them two days ago.'

'I think we'll have to leave you off the contributors' page,' she said. 'It's too late.'

The poor woman could not have been expected to understand the logistical problems of writing on the road, but I made a promise to myself that I would never go to that sort of effort again.

One of the things I dreaded was my laptop or some other bit of technology poking its tongue out at me or breaking down. It could take an extraordinary amount of time to find someone to sort it out. If we happened to be in Christchurch or Wellington it was all right. If we happened to be in a place like Tuatapere or Omarama it was a very big problem indeed.

There was, for instance, the saga of a new transformer. We were in Te Anau when I ordered it, after much research, from a supplier in Christchurch. Two weeks later it arrived but the connection was the wrong size. I sent it back and waited another two weeks, by which time we were south of Haast. I didn't trust that it would ever find me there, or feared we'd have moved on by the time it arrived. So I had it sent to poste restante in Hokitika. Ten days later it wasn't there either. I burst into tears, much to the astonishment of the Postshop staff. I thought about throwing myself into the Hokitika River. I finally traced it to Greymouth poste restante. I kissed the woman who gave it to me. She was a tall thin person with limp hair and wearing large glasses, and she looked very pleased.

In Arrowtown there was one person I was very keen to meet. Roger Hill was one of New Zealand's most decorated war veterans. He was ninety-one years of age and so there was every possibility that this would be the last chance I would get to hear his story first hand. I asked a local historian, a journalist, three shop keepers, a lodge owner and the man at the garage where I might find him. And the odd thing was that, although this man had been heralded as a great hero of World War II, talked about and written about, and people he saved had come from all over the world to thank him, not one of those I asked had heard of him. It was a librarian who finally was able to give me the phone number of one of his daughters who lived in the town.

I called her and she told me that her dad had suddenly become ill. So I had to be content with walking past the neat house and rose garden on the outskirts of the town where this extraordinary man lived. Hanging at full mast on a flag pole attached to the fence was the white ensign. Sadly, when I walked past the next day it was at half mast.

The most outstanding exploits of Lieutenant Commander Roger Hill RN, DSO, DSC happened in the Mediterranean when he was commanding the destroyer HMS *Ledbury*. When a Sunderland aircraft loaded with depth charges was downed by mistake by one of his convoy's merchant ships, he was the first to strip off his clothes and dive overboard to try and rescue the crewmen. On another occasion he sailed into a hellish inferno of black smoke and burning oil to pick up sixty-five survivors of the bombed merchant ship *Waimarama*. But most significantly he played a vital part in turning the tide of the war when he guided the crippled tanker *Ohio* into Malta, through horrendous air and torpedo attacks, to bring oil and food to a besieged island on the brink of surrender. I was genuinely sorry not to have met him.

O n Saturday night there was a big Super Twelve rugby game and Bill walked down to the town to catch the preamble on Sky at the New Orleans Bar. I followed later and, through lack of clear communication, ended up at the Royal Oak across the road. Although I was not much of a rugby follower, I liked these gatherings of the faithful in the bars of smaller places around the country. The atmosphere was smoky and cheerful, and there was a camaraderie about the shared interest. The warmth was punctuated by a jabbering of groans, cheers and spontaneous umpiring: *aaargh, off-side – yeeep, holding – oooh, advantage – aaah, penalty – go go – bloody idiot*. It had all the drama of a Southern Baptist church service.

Opposite me sat a solidly built man in a patchwork jacket so colourful it made me think of the biblical Joseph. He had constantly swivelling eyes and every now and then our gazes locked – by mistake on my part, not by intent. After the match had finished he offered to buy me a beer. I thanked him, thinking I'd swallow it politely, excuse myself and bolt for home. I told him primly, lest he had ideas, that my partner was probably in the pub on the other side of the road.

'Is his name Bully?' he said.

'No. It's Bill.'

'Ah, Billy. That's close enough. Your name wouldn't be Rosa would it?'

'No. Actually it's Jill,' I said, 'but Rosa's got a better ring to it. You can call me Rosa if you like.'

'Don't you know about Bully and Rosa?' he said. 'He was in a pub on one side of the road and she was in one on the other side. It's one of the most famous stories in Arrowtown.'

Of course I had to hear it.

'Back in the 1840s,' he said, 'Rosa Buckingham was a singer and entertainer in Aussie. Her and her whole family – she had a few brothers. I think they were quite well known. Anyway they – Rosa in particular – caught the eye of Bully Hayes. He was a nasty bit of work from all accounts but a charmer. He fancied Rosa and enticed her whole family to come with him to Dunedin and then to the Otago goldfields to perform. They ended up here in Arrowtown. The miners loved Rosa, and her brothers opened a hotel and bar for her to perform in. It was across the road somewhere, though it's long gone now. I think it was called the Provincial.

'They made a poultice of money. Bully was really green-eyed, so he opened a pub on this side of the road and called it the Prince of Wales, and he got Rosa to switch sides and perform in his pub. She obviously fancied him too. Rosa's brothers were furious. They tried everything they could to ruin Bully Hayes. One of the rumours they put around was that he'd lost an ear in a brawl. And they put up a five-pound reward if anyone could prove it. A barber won the money because he cut Bully's hair short and revealed that it was true – he only had one ear. Rosa's brothers got someone to write a comedy about it called *The Barbarous Barber*, and they put it on stage at the Provincial. I think Bully would have murdered the lot of them if it hadn't been for a storm that came through and all but demolished both hotels.'

'So what happened to Rosa?' I said, reaching for the peanuts and taking another gulp of beer.

'She went off with Bully. They went back to Australia at some stage and they had a kid, a son, I think. Then they sailed back here and somewhere up around Nelson the small boat they were in capsized and Rosa and the kid drowned, but Bully survived. He was a bit of a character I reckon, a real dirty-tempered bastard and a defrauder and rogue of the first order. He had red hair and very blue eyes. I know that much. He was also meant to be a blackbirder and a gun runner, and once I heard a fella call him a bilker and a vamooser – whatever that means.'

I bought 'Joseph' a beer and thanked him for the story. Then I vamoosed myself. It was ten o'clock by the time I'd walked home. It seemed as if the raconteur and I were the only people left in town.

Gold Shadowlands

One of the things about Central that was unavoidable was its past. There were ghost towns everywhere, many of them so ruined that it strained my imagination to conjure up their form or substance.

Bill and I drove the 15 kilometres from Arrowtown to Macetown, which sounded easy enough but turned out to be an arduous and nerve-racking journey. The track followed the Arrow River, fording it twenty-three times. When we weren't in the river we were jiggling precariously along a narrow rocky ledge that some people referred to as a road. The engine was in power thrust; my imagination was in turbo. As I visualised us plunging into the ravine 50 metres below I wondered if the whole of my life would flash before me or just the good bits.

But I trusted the Safari's power and toughness. It was the mechanical version of a draught horse, with a high carriage, sturdy tyres and grunty engine.

'We can't go through there,' I screeched as we slithered down a particularly steep shingle bank into a river full of rocks as high as cart wheels. The brakes, wet from their river dipping, started to make terrifying squealing and grinding noises and I expected that at any moment they'd give up. We ground through the clattering stream and hauled out the other side with water pouring off the

Safari. If she'd been alive I'm sure her flanks would have been heaving.

'I think you should drive on the way back,' Bill said. 'If anything happened to me in these situations you would have to, so you might as well have a go while I am here.'

Driving turned out to be easier than being a passenger because I had to do the job with such fierce concentration that it stopped any dreadful flights of fancy.

For miners and their wives and children, the trip out on foot or maybe horseback must have been appalling, and when it snowed impossible. There'd be no 'Could you just pop down to the supermarket for some eggs?' or 'Shall we eat out tonight, dear?' I wouldn't have lived up there for the pot of gold at the end of the rainbow *plus* all the tea in China.

Macetown itself was pretty well gone. Except for the reconstructed bakery building, the town was all crumbled walls and chimneys. Wild vines and bushes and the exotic trees planted by the miners would soon ensure that any sign of human presence would be wiped from the raw hills. Already we had to be told that we'd arrived by a small stone cairn with a bronze plate that stated 'This plaque marks the site of Macetown'.

We clambered around the desiccated remains of many of Central's ghost towns, places like Bendigo, Tinkers and Drybread, but the one that held by far the most appeal was St Bathans. It had a population of three, and a reasonable number of buildings were still standing so that I could wallow in bygone times without having to tax my imagination too much.

I rummaged through the ruins and buildings like a Chinaman at the tailings looking for remnants that would help me to feel its past. I found the overgrown ruins of the school with some of its Gothic windows still intact and a creeper growing prettily around the fireplace. And, sitting on a fallen stone in a classroom furnished with grass, I painted in a teacher in her corsets and long skirts and a rag-tag collection of children drawing on slates.

Near the school was the old Roman Catholic church with a graveyard full of Irish names and origins – natives of County Clare, Wicklow, Wexford, Kerry or Donegal who never made it home but maybe never intended to. Here lay the body of Samuel Turner, drowned in the river, and William Turner who was killed by a fall of earth. Other local names, though not on the gravestones, hinted at the miners' foibles. There were Charley Balloo, Jimmy the Grunter, Gory Onion and Matchmaking Mathew, as well as Ahadibox Mullock and a travelling salesmen called Barney White Rats.

Down the road was the old gaol, a one-roomed building now turned into visitor accommodation. I couldn't even lift the old ball and chain by the bed let alone escape with it strapped to my ankle. On the same plot of land was a rough corrugated-iron shed, allegedly the first building in St Bathans, which had been the dwelling for the constabulary. One hundred and fifty years later it was still standing despite the first occupant's complaint that it would fall over if a horse nudged it.

Up the road a small iron-clad church of St Alban perched on a sloping section of long grass. A notice on the wall in the porch explained that it was prefabricated in England and erected in 1883 by the founder of Dalgety's, one of the country's biggest meat producers, for the benefit of the workers on the nearby Dalgety Station.

As I was trying the door handle one-third of the St Bathans population called out a greeting from the gate.

'Gidday. How are you?'

I turned guiltily towards him.

'Keith Hinds,' he said. 'I'm sort of the honorary conservation officer and policeman around here.'

'Oh, am I trespassing?'

He laughed. 'Hardly. I thought you might have been admiring my wall.' He pointed to the dry-stone construction that divided the church property from the road.

'You built that?'

'Yep, I've done a bit of walling.'

Once, for a newspaper story, I'd made a study of the art of dry-stone walling in England, and I could see that this wall was the work of a craftsman. Keith pointed out the tie rocks for stabilising and the coping rocks on top to keep the rain off, and the accurate correlation of the base to the ridge to ensure stability.

'You gotta do it with your hands so you can feel the shape of each piece of rock and find where it fits,' he said.

Keith had been at St Bathans for seventeen years and lived in the old mine-manager's cottage. In the front room of the old weatherboard post office in the main (and only) street he ran a souvenir and knick-knack store and the village Postshop. It was crammed with early twentieth-century bric-a-brac, delicate china pieces, Victorian-style jewellery, second-hand books and stickers of coquettish little girls, of the type I can remember sticking into scrapbooks when I was about six. I was dressed in jeans but the atmosphere of the shop made me feel that a long skirt with a lace petticoat and a feathered hat might have been more appropriate. I left the shop clutching a bag of home-made aniseed balls and an old copy of *From North Cape to Bluff* by AH Reed.

The rest of the St Bathans population resided at the Vulcan Hotel (1869), which of the fourteen hotels that used to vie for customers was the only one still standing. It was made of sun-dried brick with a wooden hoarding and the carving of a shamrock over the door. The managers, Owen and Bev, had come there three years earlier from Oturehua, down the road. They served drinks in the long front bar, as well as steaks and pasta salads in a dim dining room decorated with porcelain dolls and horse tack. Around the walls of the bar were hung poems written by past patrons and old photographs of mining and sluicing. And mounted on the wall as guardians of the billiards table was a stuffed goat's head and that of a rather gruesome looking black boar.

It was a warm and reassuring pub but not overcrowded: for the first hour we were the only patrons. We warmed our toes in front of the fire box while a small dog snoozed on the window seat. A larger black dog of advancing years slept under the table and every now and then emitted malodorous wind that compelled me to hold my breath – a difficult thing to achieve when you are talking. No one else seemed to notice, or else they thought it was me and were too polite to say anything.

Bev joined the smaller dog on the window seat and lit a cigarette. She was a sturdy, good-looking blonde women, with eyes that glittered behind large glasses. I took her to be in her fifties. She was open and friendly but there was also a steeliness about her that I thought I wouldn't want to tangle with.

If there was any trouble Bev was the one to deal with it. 'If Owen tried there'd be more trouble,' she said.

I could see how that could happen. Owen was a man of visible substance who looked as if he could throw a hefty punch if provoked.

'We had one lad in here the other day who threw a billiard cue,' said Bev. 'I got him by the ear and dragged him outside. "You don't do that in my pub," I told him. His friends begged me to let him in. Well, I did after he'd cooled his heels for a bit. But he had to sit on a stool in front of the bar where I could watch him.'

I decided not to mention that her dog was farting.

Owen and Bev were both concerned about the viability of the pub. 'The owners think we're sitting in the middle of Dunedin and people will just pour through the door,' Bev said. 'But you've got to get them here in the first place.

'Today we had a bus come through and pull up in front of the pub. We sold a soda and two beers. Two ladies bought a pie and halved it and five of them came in to use the toilet. Tourists come here for a pee and a quick look around and head off again. There's no revenue in that. Some people tell us to encourage student groups here because they drink a lot, but we don't want them. Any revenue goes in damage – broken windows and chairs, you name it.

'Still, I love it here,' she said. 'You get to be your own person. I'm never lonely. You get to love the quiet of the place after a while.'

Owen, who had a ready grin and spoke with the enthusiasm of a small boy who'd been forced to stand still, was quite evidently enjoying himself. 'We have to be everything, you see – well there's nobody else. We're the ambulance service, security officers, fire chiefs as well as the publicans – everything. We had a fire the other day. There was a full turnout – me and Keith. By the time we got there the fire was out of its own accord. Since I've been here I've been called out about six times to fires. The worst was a tussock fire. Man that was frightening. The noise – the roar and the crackle even two hills away was terrific, blotted everything else out of your mind – just this huge bloody noise. It travelled any which way, faster than a man can run. Really scary I tell you.'

He took us to see the fire station, which was an elongated one-car garage. Resting on the dirt floor was Little Flick, a forty-eight-year-old red Land Rover with 5131 miles on the clock. It had all the trappings: the sirens and whistles, a red light, a search light, a ladder on the roof and a hose reel on the bonnet. Hanging in a row on the wall were five old-fashioned fireman's helmets and five woollen uniforms slowly being chewed to rags by an army of moths.

Owen pulled one off the hook. 'There were people here then,' he said. 'See the labels. Lorraine, Rachel, Larry – all gone now, though Lorraine comes here sometimes at weekends.' He tried on Larry's coat and found it wouldn't do up around his middle. 'I'd be stuffed if I'd fight a fire in these things,' he said. 'You couldn't run up a hill with all that stuff on. Get too hot. You'd bloody die.'

I couldn't help thinking that Owen with his indomitable spirit would have made a great gold miner.

'There's a water tank down the road,' he went on. 'Little Flick can pull it but it's got to be emptied out in the winter because she freezes solid. There's also a trailer full of more gear but the coupling doesn't fit the Land Rover so we have to get another vehicle to pull it.'

That evening, after our meal of steak and pasta salad in Bev's dining room, we wandered back down to the road to where we were staying. The night was clear, iron dark in the shadows, and so quiet we could have been on the moon. When we looked across to the darkened lake we almost believed we were. The village was dominated by this basin of deep still water that marked the spot where there was once a hill – before the miners sent it bit by bit down the river to the sea. It was surrounded by high white cliffs that sluicing and weathering had pinched into bizarre shapes and by day were perfectly mirrored in the glassy surface of the water.

Welshmans Gully, a few kilometres away from the largely Irish St Bathans, was named for the obvious reason. The discord between the Irish and the Welsh was legendary, breaking out into inter-town brawls on St Patrick's and St David's Days and probably many days in between. Both parties numbed their injuries in the same pub and were sometimes heard singing 'Land of my Fathers' and 'The Wearing of the Green' in a kind of harmony.

In the way that Central Otago towns all seemed to have frequently changed their names, Welshmans Gully was now called Cambrians. Like St Bathans it had a population of three. For a while it was four because Rainer Beneke, a jeweller I met in Dunedin, used to live there and buy his gold from a local miner. Now he'd shifted to the city because, he said, of his addiction to good coffee. But he went back there for weekends and I decided to go and see if he was at home.

I walked along a neatly mown grass path through the trees to a small weatherboard cabin. It was tightly shut up but I could see why he had liked the place. The house was an unpretentious hut that overlooked the bush and the white pinnacles of old tailings. Steps led to a red front door and I peered through the window to see comfortable old sofas pulled up to a large pot-belly stove. Everything was neatly stacked and organised, and out the back was a smaller building I took to be the studio. A few birds chattered in the trees. It was so peaceful that I took the liberty of lying down on Rainer's recently mown lawn, inhaling its herby smell and squinting at the sun, which seemed to be racing across the sky with a raft of white clouds in tow.

Just down the road a small mud-brick cottage demanded my attention. It was like a child's drawing, with a central door, a window on each side and smoke curling out of the chimney. At the gate was a sign with the cartoon figure of a man with a beard and a message that read 'Beware of the hug'. Feeling like Snow White I crept up the winding flagstone stone path, which was strewn with weeds. The door was open and a radio was playing. I knocked. No answer. I knocked louder. Still nothing.

I called out, 'Helloooo. Anybody home?'

No answer.

A gaggle of rust-coloured chooks came trotting around the corner of the house and gathered hopefully around me. I became bolder. I poked my head inside the door and saw a small sitting room with a fireplace, an old Singer sewing machine on one side and a cupboard on the other, and comfortable chairs gathered around it. There was an elegant figure drawing on one wall and, to my utter astonishment, a pile of brightly coloured, pointy-crowned felt hats. Then I really felt like Snow White. The sitting room seemed to lead to a kitchen and to one side a bedroom, but I couldn't will myself to step right in to the house.

I walked around the back. Nobody there either, so I wandered back out to the gate. Over in the paddock on the other side of the road a man was piling sticks into a trailer.

I yelled out to him, 'Hi there. Do you know where the man who lives in the cottage is?'

'That's Bob,' he said. 'Nope, no idea sorry. But he won't be far away.'

Ten minutes later a car pulled up beside mine and a tall slim man with long hair, bushy grey beard and a colourful pillbox hat climbed out. He gave me a dazzling smile.

'Well helloooo,' he said, as if I were a long-lost and very welcome friend. He took three strides to where I was standing, wrapped his arms around me and gave me a lingering hug. It was the most full-blooded welcome I had ever received from a stranger. But Bob was not going to be a stranger for long.

'Now,' he said, 'let's go and have a cup of tea or a glass of my home-made elderberry house wine.'

I was totally charmed. The cottage was as neat as a pin. In the kitchen there were shelves of preserves and herbs, and precisely stacked pots and plates. A kettle was already warmed on the wood stove. Bob made tea in a teapot covered in a metal cosy and brought out a tin of biscuits he'd made in the wood-fired oven. I was impressed.

'Usually there is someone passing,' he said, crinkling his blue eyes at me. 'But there was no one today – until you. Living in an outpost like this is a juggle between having space on your own and having too much space on your own. It's a long, long way from the rush of Elliott Street in Auckland to Cambrians.'

Bob, who I guessed to be in his fifties, told me he had graduated from teachers' college, then worked in Thames and eventually come south to Queenstown. I quizzed him about how he'd ended up in Cambrians.

'Well, one day a cobber of mine said, "Let's go to the Vulcan for the day." We did, and I fell in love with the mud-brick building across the road. The publican at that time owned it and when I expressed an interest he said, "Go away. Think about it and make me an offer." I ended up buying the building and I came to live in St Bathans. Then one evening a local farmer called in to have a yarn and share a bottle of beer. As we were standing talking a car flashed past. "Pretty busy round here," I said to him. He said, "I've got a little place in the country that might suit you better." That was this place. There's thirty acres of land around the house and I'm planting it in all exotic forest. I'm really excited about this project. It's become my reason for being.'

'And the hats?'

'Oh yeah, I make those. It gives me a bit of a living.'

Not a dwarf in sight.

When I was about to leave, Bob walked with me to the truck. Half way down the path he paused, lifted his hand in a gesture of supplication and said, 'I love it here. Sometimes I think I've died and gone to heaven. Look at all these autumn leaves. You see that big oak tree over there? Isn't it amazing. The only thing that ruins the perfection is that the ferrets are eating my chooks.'

'Bugger the ferrets,' I said.

'I certainly would if I could catch them.'

Over the Hill

Sometimes it was the journey rather than the destination that was the reason for taking a particular route. In the South Island the high mountain passes – Haast, Lindis, Arthur's and Lewis – led through such awesome topography that I had to remind myself to breathe. It was hard to touch the soul of these monumental landscapes through the windows of a car, even if we drove very slowly, and I sometimes dreamt about how it would be to walk or cycle or ride a donkey through them instead.

Locals and wannabe locals often refer to these amazing feats of road engineering with laconic nonchalance. 'I'm going through Arthur's,' they'd say, or 'over the Lindis' or 'up the Haast' or, as a more masterly bit of understatement, 'I'm popping over the hill.'

The 'hill' we most often popped over, by both road and rail, was Arthur's Pass. We saw the route in most of its humours: glittering with snow, in white-hot sunlight, battered by rain, sullen under threatening skies and completely fog-bound so that we couldn't see anything at all. Sometimes we did not get as far as the pass but stopped off along the way before turning back to return to the east coast or the west, depending on where we were staying at the time. At first we could not take the caravan with us because the road's condition made it impossible. We couldn't say we knew the Arthur's Pass Road like the backs of our hands, but we'd spent a lot of time pottering around various places along the route and that made it feel familiar.

From the east the interesting part always began when we left the Canterbury Plains to climb into the mountains past Porter Heights, Mt Cheeseman and Broken River ski fields. The last had particular significance for us because Bill and I had once – before the caravan time – driven through the beech trees and then climbed with the aid of crampons up the steep and crunchy slope that led to the Broken River hut, which was of the crude type that was often found on New Zealand's club skifields. It was a real problem getting luggage up this wicked little path until Clive Stevenson, the dean of the engineering school at Canterbury university, and Arthur Tyndale, a consulting engineer, devised an inclinator that climbed for 330 metres right up the 35-degree slope through the bush.

Getting from the huts to the skiable part of the mountain was not all that easy either. It was by means of a rope tow to which I clung by way of a nutcracker. Even when I managed that safely the ski slopes were, for my pitiful standard of skiing, a teeth-gritting challenge. Still I skidded around them well enough, even if not always on skis.

The view from the highest ridge was stunning. It took in a large sweep of the Craigieburn Range, the shadowed recesses of the Harper Gorge and, beyond, the snow-wrapped peaks of the Black Ranges multiplying into the distance. But the view the other way was alarming, back down the sharp slope of the skifield I had just been hauled up, which I had to face with valour in order to reach base camp again. The club manager Ross Campbell, who had urged me to that height, shouted 'Piece of cake!' as he carved smoothly off down the mountain. It was all right for him. He'd been skiing there all his life.

Walking down the mountain that night was also difficult. The snow was soft and unsupporting. At one point Bill sank into a drift up to his waist. Yelling, scrabbling at the snow with his hands and frantically jerking his body, he looked like a beetle caught in a pot of honey. I howled with laughter. We extracted him by clawing at the snow and pulling until he emerged bit by bit onto slightly more solid ice.

A few minutes later I had my comeuppance. My outside leg caught in a drift and I fell with my leg twisting at a most ungainly and painful angle. I was injured. The ski patrol couldn't get a sledge to me in that mushy snow and to this day I regret that I didn't make a fuss, that I didn't demand they call out Mountain Rescue or a helicopter or the army. Instead I had to back very slowly down the hill on a gammy knee, with Bill heroically guiding me in the dark. It took an hour and my last reserves of energy. As walking wounded I was transported off the mountain next day – by way of the inclinator like so much luggage.

At Castle Hill nature had sculpted some bizarre masonry on either side of the road. One time we turned off the road to watch a group of adventurers abseiling down the side of one of the larger ramparts of karst.

'Have a go,' said the guide.

'Not a chance.'

I had done my last ever abseil a few months earlier when I had, in a moment of bloated self-confidence, agreed to lower myself down a 90-metre cliff. When I discovered what 90 metres *looked* like my bravado drained away as fast as water down a plug hole, but I'd got too far to back out without loss of face. Launched into space I found myself in a state that rock climbers call 'stay no go'. Completely stripped of self-possession, I didn't want to go down and I couldn't go back. I felt on that fifteen-minute descent like a terrified, out-of-control spider.

. . .

We travelled right over Arthur's Pass on the day before the Otira Viaduct opened. We had parked the caravan in Ashburton so that we could drive over the old road on the last day it was open and back on the first day of the new.

The astonishment we felt when we first drove over the state-of-the-art engineering marvel, which snaked like a piece of modern sculpture through the Otira Gorge, was not so much about where we were then as where we had been the day before. I looked back up the huge, 2000-year-old fan of scree spilling down the side of the mountain and located the scar of the old road carved across the face of it.

I knew that my great-grandfather Harvey had travelled the original road, over that precarious ledge, in a Cobb & Co. carriage about four years after its 1866 construction. I had crossed it in a Nissan Safari in 1999, but my feeling of awe and apprehension as we wound around the narrow, steep, avalanche-prone switch-back from Starvation Point to Deaths corner would most likely have been the same as his.

In all the hype for the opening of the viaduct there was not much tribute paid to the men who built that old road. They'd had the same bitter elements to contend with and few of the advantages provided by modern facilities and technology. In 1865 a thousand men with axes, picks, shovels, crowbars, wheelbarrows, rock drills and explosives headed for the hills. There they toiled the year long, in atrocious conditions, to carve the road out of the near-impossible terrain by scarfing cliff faces and reinforcing dodgy embankments with walls made of timber cribbing filled with blocks of stone.

On our last drive over their handiwork, Bill and I had pulled off the road at the top of the steep haul up the gorge and applauded their gumption. It was a memorable pause weighted with the passing of history. Because it was in a national park, the old road was to be broken up and the bush allowed to regenerate. The legacy of the thousand would sink unsung into the landscape.

. . .

About a year later on a weekend trip to Greymouth we pulled in to the High Country Wilderness Lodge to stay the night. It was the year of the great drought and all across the plains and hills of Canterbury the grasslands had turned a pale sickly yellow, while the foothills of Mt Horrible, adjacent to the lodge, had been blackened by fire. Helicopters like large black hornets, with monsoon buckets attached to their underbellies, were still patrolling. In a paddock adjacent to the lodge, fire headquarters had been set up. Outside a caravan, sitting on box, a fireman was reading the paper.

'Is the fire still going?' I called out, waving a hand towards the helicopters.

'Could be,' he said, 'although we think it's pretty much out. But fire can live in the trunk of a burnt tree. It can even burn away down in its roots for a week or more and then suddenly burst out again. So we're not taking any chances, that's for sure.'

It was comforting, considering our proximity. I didn't fancy frying in my bed.

The Arthur's Pass Wilderness Lodge was created by Gerry McSweeney and his wife Anne to give people a wilderness experience from a place of comfort. Another aim was to demonstrate that it's possible to have profitable, up-market accommodation and environmental integrity at the same time. Nine years earlier I had worked with Gerry on the Ecotourism Awards and since then I had become one of his converts.

As we drove into the parking area and stopped among the beech trees, Gerry was there with his nose poked into the bushes. He was surrounded by a group of young Japanese boys peering intently in the same direction.

'How are you doing Gerry?' I called.

He looked up and without preamble said, 'Come over here and see what we're up to.'

This turned out to be mistletoe seeding, which involved sticking the seeds of the plant to tree trunks, where they could germinate.

'Birds usually do this,' he said. 'They eat the berries and wipe the seeds off their beaks onto the branch, but mistletoe is disappearing because possums love to eat the seeds. So we're giving them a bit of a hand.'

Gerry was so enthusiastic about the miracles of plant life that it rubbed off. He was one of the most focused, energetic and argumentative people I knew. He was a man who stuck to his guns and his principles – one of those people who never seemed to flinch in the face of fierce opposition.

While Bill went out the next morning on a guided walk, I walked through the quiet beech forest on my own. At least I thought I was alone – and then on a low branch I saw a kea, silent and still, with its head slightly cocked checking on my progress. When it realised it was spotted, it spread its wings to flash their brilliant orange undersides, uttered a hideous cackle and buzzed me, flying low enough to make me duck. I watched it join two others on the forest floor and they all began tearing into a rotten log with their formidable beaks. Recently I'd seen a British television documentary in which keas had been proclaimed the most intelligent animals on earth on account of their ability to solve complex practical problems. I suspected they also had a sense of humour.

Our last trip over Arthur's was in April 2001, just before the drive became even smoother with the opening of the Candys Bend project, which widened part of the road and built a robust concrete rock shelter over it to protect vehicles from falling debris. But the day we drove it the section was still one way and things were not going at all smoothly. As we came up to Candys Bend the scene that greeted us was one of helicopters, squashed cars, ambulances and police cars, and everybody dashing to and fro, too busy to pass on information. We kept well out of it and let them do their jobs.

It wasn't until the next day we found out had happened. A truck carrying 25 tonnes of hotmix had gone out of control on the viaduct, hurtled down the one-way section of the gorge as workmen dived for cover, and ploughed into three cars that were making their way up the road in the opposite direction. The report said that when the truck driver managed to stop his vehicle 'he promptly jumped out of the cab and vomited', which was hardly surprising. Miraculously, *really* miraculously considering the state of one car that had been squashed to a wheelbarrow-sized chunk of mangled metal, nobody was hurt.

Eventually a rotund little man in a stiff yellow raincoat and helmet waved us through a gap in the gradually clearing mayhem. Sobered and aghast at the possible consequences of what we had seen, we drove with great caution. A passenger bus passed us going the other way. The driver spread his fingers in a matey kind of wave. Two minutes later he ran out of brakes above the one-way section and smashed into the rock wall just below Candys Bend. It was another miracle: there were twenty-one people on board and only one needed medical attention – to stop the bleeding from a scratch on the leg.

'I think we'll put Arthur's on hold for a while,' Bill said, and the next time we popped over the hill to the West Coast we took the spectacular route over the Haast Mountains to the south.

Wriggilus Evadus

We arrived at Haast Beach Motor Camp the day after the worst flood anyone there could remember. It had been a soft fine day on our side of the divide and, although great scuds of cloud had greeted us as we topped the pass and began our descent, nothing warned us of the deluge on the coast that had sent the rivers howling down their channels and spreading sheets of water over the lowland.

Maybe we just hadn't noticed. We had our own problems. Just after we had dropped 450 metres from the pass, we'd hung out the windows to check on the caravan and were horrified to see great puffs of smoke erupting from somewhere near its wheels. We pulled off the road as soon as there was room and discovered that the over-worked brakes were glowing red hot. Another kilometre or two and the whole caboodle could have burst into flames. We waited while they cooled, disconnected them and went the rest of the way on the engine brake, controlling our speed with great care.

So it was something of a surprise to arrive at the camp and find that even the parts that were still habitable were as soggy as a green sponge. In the misty half light at the end of the day it felt as if we were setting up in the marshes of Mordor. No sooner had the jacks settled into the slosh than there was a commanding rap on the door and there stood not an elf but a stout middle-aged woman in a bright pink track-suit and with sparkling clips in her hair. In her arms she carried a huge, floppy, long-haired cat.

'Grab your meat and come on over for a barbie,' she said. 'We're all getting together tonight for a bit of a do.'

The camp was full of whitebaiters who went there every year in August and stayed until about mid-November. They built their rigs out into the river and set their nets every high tide, but I suspected they were there as much to catch the camaraderie and good times as they were to net the whitebait.

'I don't even eat the stuff,' one man at the barbie confided, biting into a half-cooked sausage, 'but I love the buzz of catching them and workin' out where the little critters will be running next. It's the thrill of the chase I guess. We call the species of whitebait you get around here wriggilus evadus. I'll tell you what, we really have some fun.'

We threw our chops onto the communal grill and joined the group of about thirty whitebaiters. The talk was 'flood'. Some people's rigs had been smashed to pieces and carried out to sea by the weight of the water. Silt had swept through a caravan down by the river and left it lined with slime. But the mood was jocular. This, I was assured, was all part of whitebaiting. The good and the bad.

'Everyone will pitch in and help and get things going again tomorrow,' said the lady in pink. 'Tonight we're gonna have fun.'

These people met every year from all over the South Island. A schoolteacher and her husband came from Invercargill and two hoteliers from south of Christchurch, but it would have been unseemly to query the backgrounds of the rest. They were there to enjoy the moment, and that meant leaving their personal stories behind.

One woman with a strong Dutch accent yelled across the group to Bill, 'Hey, get those trousers off, I want to see your legs. You should've left your shorts on. You've got great legs. Saw them when you came in.'

The woman from Invercargill huddled closer to me. 'You mustn't mind her,' she said. 'She's always like that.'

I didn't mind at all.

The camp proprietors came and handed round cheese on toast. I asked one woman, who had a lot of hard history scribbled on her face, if she had her own stand. It was, apparently, a thunderclap of tactlessness.

'Well, of course I bloody do. Whaddaya think I'm here for?' She leant forward with her elbows on her knees and looked me hard in the eyes. 'So where'd you come from?' It was a challenge as much as a question.

'Auckland.'

'Dorkland. Oh yeah yeah. Where's that?' She laughed harshly and rolled her eyes towards the group, trying to gain complicity.

I ignored her.

I was fed up with these sorts of stabs about being an Aucklander, as if I were a foreigner in my own country. At first I'd taken them in good part, but my tolerance was wearing thin. This attitude, which happily seemed to be on the decline, betrayed an anxiety that the deliverer just might be missing out on something but was powerless to go and see if it were true.

There were others who were utterly content to be where they were, and they had a quite different attitude. As far as they were concerned, God had made their particular part of the world and merely coloured in the rest. They knew without a quiver of doubt that they were in the best place, and therefore had no need to be snide about other places or even look any further afield. Although such certainty could be seen as limited, I found it reassuring. Among the dissatisfaction and lack of permanence in a modern world it was good to find some hardy souls whose identity was forged by an enviable sense of place.

I liked the pink lady. She had a robust sense of humour and a way of making the most of everything. We shared an addiction to *Coronation Street* and discussed the cast as if they were mutual friends. This led her to rush to her caravan and bring back a photograph that she showed me with a mixture of mirth and pride. It was a picture of herself, again in pink and holding her cat, standing between the people who played Hayley and Roy, two of the Street's main characters. She'd spotted them in the camping ground a few nights before and certainly wasn't going to let an opportunity like that pass her by.

The day after the barbecue, Bill and I went down to the Turnbull River to inspect the damage. Outside a small cabin, two men had spread their belongings on the ground to dry. Don and Ian were over from Wanaka. They'd woken up on the night of the flood to find water swirling ankle-deep through the cabin.

'We made a decision to get out while we still could,' Don told us. 'Especially when we looked outside and saw that water was already up to the running board of my four-wheel-drive. We abandoned the cabin on the double and waded to the car to drive it and us to higher ground.

'You'd have noticed that the track you just came down dips before it leads up to the road from the riverbank. Well, that was bad enough, but I think we also went into a ditch of some sort because in next to no time the water had risen as high as the dashboard, the vehicle had stalled and all the electrics jammed. Neither the doors nor the windows would open. We were in a helluva mess.'

I glanced at the four-wheel-drive, which now had all its doors open to dry. It still looked decidedly soggy inside. Weed dribbled from its running boards and bumpers.

'I heaved myself into the back,' Don continued, 'to find the jack that I knew was lying around somewhere. And I managed to raise it above my head enough to bring it down against the driver's window. The glass shattered.'

There'd been no one to witness the two sodden men, clad in their underpants, emerge like writhing sandworms from the driver's window and make their way through the water to higher ground.

Don ran to the nearest house and roused the owner, who obligingly appeared at the scene with his tractor. Don dived under the churning water and somehow attached a rope to his vehicle, hoping to have it towed to dry land or at least to stop it from sailing on out to sea.

'I came up from the dive,' he said, 'wearing mud and river weed and looked up to the bridge to see the bedraggled figure of Ian gazing down at me in a dazed sort of way with blood from cuts made by the glass running in decorative streaks down his legs.'

Forty-eight hours later things were almost back to normal. The car had been cleaned up and serviced at the garage down the road. Back at the cabin bacon was cooking on the gas hob and a cup of tea was on offer. Two pairs of mud-coloured underpants were drying in the watery sun on a bush that grew on the banks of the river.

I liked the unruliness of this corner of the South Island. The beach was about twenty minutes' walk from the camp. To describe it as wild was an even wilder understatement. Great, booming, terrifying waves thumped and swirled up the beach in a fury. Bleached tree trunks littered the grey sand and, shrouded in spray 5 kilometres offshore, were the Open Bay Islands. These had been a base for sealers in earlier days. They lived out there to get away from the constant harassment of mosquitoes and sandflies on the mainland, even though they had to contend with the sea and armies of New Zealand's only known land leeches.

In early 1810 the brig *Active* put ten sealers ashore on one of the islands with orders to collect and cure as many skins as possible, while it sailed to Sydney and back. The ship was never heard of again. By the end of the year the men had collected 11,000 skins but they had a bit of a problem. Their own boat, their only means of communication with the mainland, had been lost in a storm. They managed to construct some flimsy sealskin canoes and made a few desperate forays across that monstrous bit of sea in an attempt to locate ships or food, but it wasn't until 1813 that contact was somehow made with a schooner that had put in to Jackson Bay. The ten sealers were rescued along with what skins were left. Apparently there were still some ruins out there but the island had returned to the seals.

I picked up a hitching crayfisherman in white gumboots and a homespun jersey, with the uniform beanie on his head. He was from the fishing village of Hannahs Clearing, just down the road, and was going to visit a friend for a few beers.

'There's nothin' much else to do around here,' the young man said.

'It must be pretty wild out there sometimes,' I said. 'Do you go near those islands?'

'Yeah, we set our pots around there when the weather's a bit quieter. It's not too bad.'

He'd never heard the story of the sealers and said he didn't go much for seals.

On the other side of the road from the camp the Hapuka estuary cut into the typical West Coast forest of kowhai, manuka, kahikatea and flax. The towering trees were festooned with perching lilies and orchids or shrouded in kiekie and rata vines. We could enter the swamp by means of an extensive boardwalk. The water of the estuary was rich in nutrients, and all native land and sea life – including whitebait – was safe in this sanctuary. I stopped to look deeply into still, dark water that, with its yeasty yellow scum around its edges, reminded me of Monteith's Dark Ale. A swim here was highly undesirable.

Bill had walked on ahead and as I hurried to catch up I heard barking noises and came around a bend to see him baying at a tree, holding his camera up to his eye with one hand and vigorously patting his head with the other.

'What on earth?'

'Shhhhhhhh!'

A kereru was sitting on a branch a few metres in front of him. He'd been trying to get a photo of one in flight for the last six months. This bird struck a righteous pose and refused to budge. I joined in the barking and head patting. Still 'stay no go'. Bill lowered the camera briefly to give me instructions. The pigeon lifted its head in the air, spread its wings and launched itself skyward with the grace of an overweight ballerina.

As a souvenir of Haast Beach and the Hapuka estuary, we now had a perfectly executed photograph of a pigeon's tail in flight.

It would be a mistake to come this far south and not continue the 25 kilometres or so to Jackson Bay, which for all practical purposes was at the farthest reach of the West Coast road.

Jackson had a population of about ten – but it once had a grand plan. There were still traces of an attempted settlement of the 1870s. After it had dished out the full scale of human misery and despair the idea foundered. Now the bush had reclaimed the grazing land so resolutely cleared by the pioneers, some of whom lay in the isolated graveyard. A handful of hardy houses still existed and a long wharf served commercial fishing boats working the wild stretch of water from Greymouth to Bluff.

We spent some time at Jackson, arriving first on a fine day when the light was good and the water in the bay gently undulating. The temperature was cold in the shade. A fisherman had just tied his boat to a buoy and rowed ashore with his mate. I walked down the old wooden wharf to the pier, stuffing my hands into the pockets of my jacket to keep them warm.

'Any luck?' I asked.

'Nah,' he said. 'It's blowing real bad out there. You see those lumps?' He pointed to the horizon. ''Tis a sou'westerly does that. Blows like hell. That's why we came in. We thought, Bugger this. We haven't caught much. We'll go out tomorrow if she's clear.'

He said his name was Fang. When he smiled, which he did disarmingly, one front tooth was missing. He was a slim boy-man who I would have guessed to be about twenty, and a tight black jersey and fitting black trousers only made him look thinner. His hair was matted and stuck out in rats' tails from his head. A large pair of sunglasses held together in the middle with sticking plaster was wrapped around his face and made him look like a fly.

He and his mate had rifles slung over their shoulders.

'We're off up the hill for a bit of a hunt. There's plenty of venison up there,' Fang said. 'We'll bag some and take it home.'

Not far out a very tidy little boat with a white-and-green hull bobbed up and down on its mooring. A man climbed over the side and rowed a dinghy to the wharf, where another man with a good haircut and hands that were too soft to be those of a fisherman was waiting beside his truck. He looked a bit like a young Michael Caine. On the back of the truck was a hoist. 'Michael' lowered a steel cable over the side of the wharf and attached it to the dinghy, which was then winched out of the water with the rower still aboard and lowered onto the back of the truck.

'Tomo' was written in large black letters at the upper rim of each of the boatman's white boots. He'd just been working on a damaged tuna line, he told me.

'Has it been a good year?' I asked.

'The tuna's been great. We've been selling it at three thousand dollars a tonne. It was half that last year. I know that sounds pretty good, but we get three dollars a kilo for stuff that probably sells for twenty in the shops. Fishermen are at the wrong end of things for the money.'

'Must be easier ways to earn a living.'

'Yeah, well, you gotta love the lifestyle to do it. You'd never do it for the money.'

'What's so good about the lifestyle?' I said, glancing towards the angry sea.

'It's the freedom,' said Tomo. 'I know we've got all these rules and levies and licences and things on land, but once you're out there down the coast you're on your own. No one can touch you. I was a meat inspector before, and then I went fishing in Fiordland. I loved it, but it was too damned cold. So when we bought our own boat we came north to Hannahs Clearing.'

'So you're frightened and freezing out there but you're free?'

'Nah, not me. I don't go out if it's really bad weather, and I've got a heated cabin, a microwave, television – you name it. I'm not into the rough stuff.'

Way out on the water was the black silhouette of a fishing boat the size of a peapod. I could see it rhythmically lifting above the level of the horizon and then sinking out of sight. It took an hour to come in to the bay and it looked like one hell of a journey.

The *Erynne Kay* was no beauty, a blunt-snouted boat with rust running down from her gunnels and an orange-coloured deck blotched with oil and dirt. The crew anchored her out in the bay and started to gut the catch. They were surrounded by a cloud of begging seagulls and two slender-winged mollymawks. When the *Erynne Kay* finally came alongside the wharf, her gruesome cargo of ling, bluenose, gurnard and blue cod was winched, bucket by bucket, onto a waiting truck to be taken to the Ngai Tahu fisheries at Neils Beach. The ling was particularly monstrous looking: floppy, elongated and pink, like an anaemic entrail.

On a bank above the beach just up from the wharf perched a trailer about 10 metres long and rather in need of a coat of paint. This was the Lobster Pot, where Dale Atkinson and her daughter Lisa, who was married to Gutty Rogers, had set up a fish and chips shop. There was no problem with supplies and, during the summer, no problem with demand. The trailer used to be the diner in Cromwell and was hauled there over Haast Pass. Inside it was divided into high-backed cubicles and through small, smeared windows you could look out to the bay. Bill and I ordered blue cod in batter with chips.

Three men came in off their tuna boat. They couldn't have been much more than thirty and already their skin had that grizzled look of sea-hardened mariners.

'Were lookin' for a good feed,' said one, rubbing his hands together in anticipation.

'Bloody wicked out there.'

I'd have thought they'd have had their fill of fish. But they ordered enough, with chips, to fill a bucket, and bent over the table shovelling it in with hands unwashed from their own fishy slaughter, concentrating and chewing hard. They had been so long in each other's company they had their own system of communication, which had shrunk to a kind of clubby Morse code. Every now and then one of them would utter a grunt or a key phrase like 'possum grub' and they'd grin as one and then carry on chewing.

'We could get like that,' I said to Bill.

He grinned. 'We already have,' he said.

A Wee Bit Wet

The West Coast was too rich a place to be swallowed whole: it had to be ingested slowly so that it could be savoured bit by bit. And the weather dictated how much you could nibble along the way. The coast was a hard place to get to know if every time you put your foot out the door it was savaged by freezing winds, sheeting rain and sandflies that bit like rats. But then one day you woke up and the rain was gone and the wind had dropped and it was as benign as a garden in spring. The trees ceased to drip and the grass verges of the road steamed with humidity as the sun dried off the land.

And so our experiences of the coast came in snatched and disjointed episodes that became implanted in the memory like a collection of blown-up photographs.

It was a perfect day at Lake Moeraki, 30 kilometres north of Haast. The sun was out, the sky was an even blue and the wind had become lazy and indifferent. Bill and I seized the moment. He went off with his camera and I obtained the loan of a small kayak, launched it from the front garden of the Moeraki Wilderness Lodge and began to paddle up the Blue River out onto the lake.

The river was hardly true to its name. The water was as black as molasses, its surface so perfectly still that I could gaze into it and see perfectly replicated the upside-down tops of the trees that crowded the river bank. Occasionally, deep down, I glimpsed a drowned twig or leaf working its way gently towards the sea – the only indication that the water was very slowly on the move. There was no sound, no titter through the trees. Nothing. The suspense was palpable, and when the clear sharp call of a bellbird cut through the silence it made me jump.

In a dazed reverie I stroked my way out onto the lake, where a stiff little breeze rippled the water's surface and ruffled through the reeds and flaxes of its margins. Stands of kahikatea stood sentinel at the base of pinched foothills, and up behind them rose the snow-dusted tip of Munro Peak. I had the extraordinary sensation that my definition of self was dissolving. I seemed to expand to become an integral part of everything around me.

I paddled back from the lake and eulogised the experience to Bill as he was photographing paradise ducks. We decided to walk from Lake Moeraki to the sea and back along Munro's Track, before the light of the afternoon ran out. 'We'll have to do this at a reasonable clip if we want to get back before dark,' Bill said.

But the bush won us over. Our appreciation of the exquisite beauty of the ferns, rocks, liverworts, mosses, spleenworts and lichens could not be hurried. If I looked up I could watch light and shadow flickering on foliage that nodded, swayed or shivered at the command of a light afternoon breeze. Lower down, tree branches were hung with ferns so delicate they were almost translucent, and everywhere the foliage glistened as if it had just been polished. If I peered closely at the forest floor I found tiny berries, orchids and fungi in the thick carpet of moss and baby ferns. From any angle every square metre of the forest presented a design so harmonious that no landscaper could ever hope to replicate it.

Away from the track the undergrowth was too dense for my gaze to penetrate far at all. I wondered how explorers, who didn't even know where they were going, ever managed to bush bash their way through stuff like this. It must have taken enormous patience to struggle just a few hundred metres. I felt a surge of gratitude for the path makers who made our present route to the sea almost effortless.

On the walk back I was still in a state of reverential wonder when a leggy German couple came towards us. They were striding through the forest with their heads down and their voices raised. We stopped to exchange greetings.

'It's absolutely magic, this place,' I said. 'God lives here. There's no sign of the devil.'

'Ja?'

Their smiles faded and I could feel they had mentally moved away even before they walked on.

'Well, I only read the book because I knew her. It was an odd sort of book. Dunno what I thought of it but it must be good if it won that prize.'

The man and his wife were sitting on the bleak and stony beach at Okarito. They'd driven a four-wheel farm bike down to the edge of the water and wrapped themselves in blankets. They'd cast their lines into the empty sea. 'To catch shark,' he said.

I queried this.

'Oh yes, we catch them all right. They're okay to eat if they're young. Yeah, we've caught a few. We've been coming here for about eight years now. We only live up the coast about an hour but we've got a little place down here. Great to get away.'

I wondered what exactly they were getting away from. Okarito, particularly in this grey dull weather, was not an alluring place.

'It's much nicer in the summer,' they said.

'Have *you* read her book?' he asked.

'Yes I have. I thought it was original, very strong and quite sinister.'

'Oh well, yeaaas. I guess so. You know we've been coming here all that time and we've never really spoken to her. We wave to each other now but that's all. She's pretty private – different I would say. Mind you, she does a lot for the community here. You'd have to say that she's right behind the community.'

They pointed out Keri Hulme's house to me, a small weatherboard place half hidden by flax bushes and a high wooden fence. On the gate by the road was a home-made sign. Its message was clear. 'Unknown cats and dogs will be shot on sight. Unless I know you or you have contacted me first do not come in. Kia ora.' That's fair enough, I thought, if you've done something noteworthy but don't particularly want to be the subject of people's curiosity for the rest of your life.

I walked along beside the sea and the atmosphere was straight out of Keri Hulme's novel *the bone people* and onto the beach – a huge dismal landscape of driftwood, like pale bones on the sand. Apart from the fishing couple there was nobody there.

At night Okarito was eerie. The wind moaned in from the sea. A grey mantle of cloud pressed down on the land and at intervals came the sound of a harsh primeval bird call. I thought it might have been a kiwi. I passed through the little straggle of buildings that made up the village and chilled myself with the possibility that the wind was the ghost sighs of the people who had walked those streets and frequented the twenty-five hotels and three theatres that were once part of the town.

The camping ground was rudimentary and cost just $5 a night. It was run by the local community, which numbered about twenty-two. A hostel in the tiny old school house was $10 a night. Bunks lined its walls and it was neat and clean and quaint. Other accommodation was at Tony and Rose-Anne's place – the Royal Motel, Hostel and 'Hutel'. Rose-Anne showed me through the two houses that she ran as backpacker hostels. They were clean and simply furnished, and there was a soft toy on each bed.

'Tom and I live in the caravan out the back,' said Rose-Anne, 'because it makes more room for the kids.'

She took a motherly interest in her 'kids'. She strode around in a big pair of boots as she showed me through, tidying and clucking disapprovingly at towels awry and the odd bit of peeling paint.

Out the back a corrugated-iron shed had been turned into an all-purpose gathering place. A large log burner was sizzling in one corner. The room was cluttered with odd collections that included a row of rugby shirts and rugby boots. Four girls, their skins rosy from the heat, were curled up in old armchairs watching television. They looked up and smiled at me vacantly and went back to watching the programme.

'The Highlanders and the All Blacks,' Rose-Anne said, seeing me looking at the jerseys. 'They're my passion. What's yours?'

I went blank. 'Ummm, oh just living,' I said lamely.

She looked at me pityingly. 'Yeah, oh I see. Anyway come on over and have an amber.'

Later I wrote in my notebook, 'Remember to live passionately.'

Driving north after our first visit to Okarito the rain caught up with us with such force that we had to shout to be heard, and seeing anything ahead was almost impossible. We crawled along the road with our lights blazing, blinking into the river that ran down the windscreen. Then ahead of us through this watery curtain Bill picked up, faintly at first and then growing stronger, the yellow glow of a light.

'What's that? There on the left?' he shouted.

The light did not move and as we came closer we saw a figure silhouetted against its beam waving both arms in the air as if he were directing an aeroplane to dock. We stopped and an utterly drenched human being sloshed up to the driver's window. Water had clamped a tousled mop of hair to his head and rivulets cascaded down his face. He was limping slightly.

'Could you give us a hand, mate?' he said. 'I'm in the bloody ditch. Shot right off the bloody road. I musta gone off to bloody sleep.'

'You okay?'

'Yeah, I think so. Bit of a bump on me leg but the rest's hunky dory as much as I can make out. Could you unhitch that van and give us a tow, mate.'

He added as an afterthought, 'The handbrake's gonna kill me.'

'Handbrake?'

'That's me wife.' He lifted his lips in something like a grin. 'She was expecting me home about an hour ago.'

Unhitching the caravan in this weather on a narrow road where visibility was nil was out of the question. We were a good 70 kilometres from Haast and at least another 50 to Fox Glacier.

'We can give you a lift up to Fox,' I said. 'I've got a cellphone. As soon as we're in range you can ring your hand…wife.'

There was a pause. Water dripped steadily off his chin. 'Nah, I'm not leavin' me car here for some bastard to pinch me tyres and radio. I'll take me chances.'

'We'll let them know in Fox,' Bill said.

'No worries. She'll be right. Thanks for stopping,' he said. 'Be bloody careful on this road, mate.' He ducked his head and looked across at me. 'Keep your powder dry.'

About 20 kilometres further on we flagged down a man driving south in a Land Rover and relayed the story.

'Okay,' he said, as if we were asking him to pick up some milk on the way home. 'No worries, I'll give him a tow when I get there. Box o' fluffies, mate.'

That episode underlined that a way of life still existed among those expanses of coastal wilderness where free-wheeling self-reliance was a hallowed tradition and physical toughness was considered to be the measure of a man. One of the ways to impress your fellows was to master the art of understatement. A serious blow to a leg was referred to as 'a bit of a bump'. A raging sea became 'kinda lumpy'. A man could struggle for two days through a freezing, rocky wilderness and refer to the expedition as 'a tad rough'. One time on the coast an articulated road colossus pulled in to a service station where we were filling up with diesel. The driver unfolded from the cab and jumped to the ground. He nodded in my direction. 'Wee bit wet,' he said by way of a greeting.

It had been pouring with rain for the last three weeks.

The Point of Going

I liked Greymouth. A lot of people didn't, but I thought it had character. The more time I spent there, the more I was taken with the brave face it put on when the sky was hanging over it as black as coal dust and the weather came pounding in from the sea threatening to swallow the whole town, lock stock and barrel.

Trembling with cold, I stood on the wharf on one such a day. There was a 3-metre swell and huge perilous-looking waves crashed in against the rocky embankment. I was astonished to see a small fishing boat come chugging down the river, pause, and then plunge clumsily across the churning bar on which many boats had foundered and head on out to sea. It seemed like risky sea-faring to me but it epitomised the snook that the town cocked to the elements.

A fisherman facing the cold in a white T-shirt was standing alongside me smoking a rollie.

'Man, that was dangerous,' I said to him.

'Nah,' he said, inhaling deeply. 'She's sweet. A bit splashy maybe, but I've been out in far worse than that.'

We also liked the camping ground in Greymouth. It was separated from the ocean by a bank of grass and we'd chosen a spot that was sheltered by trees. Nobody much was around in the winter but we were visited each evening by an inquisitive weka that nosed around looking for booty. It fell upon the piece of tinfoil I offered as if it were a winning Lotto ticket, sprinting off with long loping strides with the treasure gripped in its beak.

My regard for the town was also coloured by one of those chance encounters that come along at the right moment to offer you something that you need. I'd been buying supplies at the supermarket and had walked to the sea frontage. It was ten in the morning, and clouds hung in the sky like grey dishcloths, looking as though they'd be dumping at any moment. I was feeling rather grey and shabby myself as I sat on a bench surrounded by plastic bags. It was the anniversary of the day Rachel had left New Zealand seven years earlier and I couldn't get what had happened to her out of my mind.

'You look like you've lost your wallet or something?'

I turned to my interrogator, a stout woman in her late thirties in an orange sweater and torn jeans, who despite her age carried signs of puppy fat around her jaw line. Her right eyebrow was pierced with a small silver bone.

'Is it that obvious?'

She shrugged. 'It's gonna rain,' she said. 'You on your own?' She had no trouble launching into personal territory.

'Well, at this very moment, yes. But I've got a partner.'

'You been divorced then?'

'Yes, a long time ago. Are you married yourself?'

'I'm not,' she said. 'Not now. He left me and the kids about three years ago. He wasn't much of a father when he lived with me and we're friends now. So that worked out for the best.'

'And how many kids do you have?' I asked her.

'Six. Well, there *were* six. My eldest died three years ago. She was sixteen.' She stated it as a matter of simple fact, with no embellishments.

'So did mine,' I said. 'She was twenty-three.'

The woman looked at me, squinting a little in the light, but it was still a strong, forthright connection.

'Tough, isn't it. Bloody tough. Still I've got my five. You got other kids?'

'Yes, two.'

'That's great. Two out of three's not bad. Tom – that's my third – he's in prison at the moment. Silly kid sold some dope. He should have smoked it himself. And Muriel my youngest, she's got this lung disease. She might not live very long either. Still, I reckon that what you're dished up is what you're dished up.' She laughed and her whole body jiggled. 'Dished up is right. That's what I do for a living. I wash dishes in this restaurant. Suits me fine. I like it.'

I looked at this plain woman with her red hands and stringy hair and imagined a life that was probably numbingly dull. There was not the slightest hint of bitterness or self-pity in her eyes. She was unbeaten, unfailingly cheerful.

We exchanged smiles.

'You want a hand with those parcels?' she said.

'I'll be fine,' I said. She'd already relieved me of some of my baggage. I packed the groceries into the car and drove back to camp in a different frame of mind. And then I remembered I hadn't even asked her name.

Greymouth was the springboard for other places on the West Coast. To the north was Westport, a town I found more difficult to love. We stayed for two days at Carters Beach, near Cape Foulwind, hoping for the rain to stop. It didn't; the only photograph I managed to get of Westport is of people scurrying around like hunched beetles to get themselves out of the rain. I promised myself that we'd spend more time there one day, in fine weather, and try to get under its skin.

I suspected that my Reverend great-grandfather had a tough assignment in this town. Back in the 1860s, as well as the weather, it would have been suffering all the bawdy debauchery and godlessness that prevailed in the country's goldfields. In the three years that he wrestled with the Devil there he must have seen plenty that disturbed him, but only one story from that period survived. It was about the time a tidal wave struck the town, undermining a lot of the buildings and sweeping them out to sea. There was an account of the incident in a book called *Harvey Come Quick*. It described the minister working with other men to salvage possessions when he saw four hotels leave their foundations and sail past him.

The Golden Hope moved off at 3 pm. precisely – wet or fine, the Reverend watch was always reliable. The National Hotel quietly slipped into the river, when the section on which it stood crumbled away and then, after colliding with Captain Riley's vessel, *The Three Friends*, collapsed on the bar. The Waterloo followed tentatively but Yates's hotel sailed out over the bar as though to the manner born. Yates himself turned to the Vicar with a certain pride. 'Doesn't she ride the waves gracefully?' he said.

The road between Westport and Karamea was a dramatically wild part of the West Coast scenery – if you could see it. First we drove through Granity. Smoke from the coal fires in the little cottages that lined the road puffed out of the chimneys to mingle with the fog. It didn't look like a good omen for better weather. We drove north under leaden skies, past brown, muttering rivers and lonely, shabby farmhouses. Isolated nikau palms stood sentinel in paddocks of bog where herds of Friesian cows crammed together with their backsides to the wind.

Three miles short of Karamea we pulled into the holiday park, in a stand of trees beside an estuary and close to the sea. The place was deserted, the steadily dripping trees turning the ground into marshland. John, who ran the camping ground with his wife Margaret, came sloshing over to greet us.

'Bloody awful weather,' he said. 'Still, it can only get better.'

I didn't believe him.

John and Margaret had come there from Nelson several years earlier.

'We love it,' John said, with water dripping off the end of his nose. 'You meet all sorts. Some foreigners come back here every year and then there's the whitebaiters. We have *such* a good time with them. Same crowd every time. You know, we nearly cry when they go. It's so desolate for a while.'

Bill and I climbed into waterproof jackets and walked to the ocean. The hills behind us were wool-textured humpy shadows with the heads of great matai trees standing up like giant broccoli. An all-wild sea slammed against the shoreline, swirling up the beach spewing whipped-cream lumps of foam onto the sand, where it sat in great piles quivering in the wind. It was a violent sea, full of rage. The trees by the beach, straining away from the fury, were bent almost at right angles. We leaned into the wind and struggled back to the caravan, got our jacks down and set, and drove to the village for supplies.

The Karamea Store was one of the last general stores in the country. On the store's old weatherboard flank a painted sign said 'Karamea Stores – Hardware and Variety', and under the bull-nose verandah a notice announced the store was 'Customarily Open'. Red post boxes were set in to one wall and nearby was a notice that explained that Maree would no longer hand mail out over the counter.

It was warm inside the store and it smelt of paper and dust. The floor was of wooden planks, grey and scuffed with age. High shelving around the walls and criss-crossing the room formed a maze that was stuffed with an assortment of the day-to-day things that one might need in that remote part of the island.

There were no computer parts, cellphones or designer labels, but there was a good range of gumboots, paint and garden tools. There were reading glasses, sou'westers, ice trays, corks, teapots, hot-water bottles, knitting wool, socks, buckets and mouse-traps. A violin concerto was playing on the radio as change rattled in the drawer till and local people came scurrying in out of the rain to make their purchases.

More interesting than the merchandise were the snippets of local gossip that floated around the aisles. I ear-wigged, skulking behind a shelf of home-spun jerseys and tartan shirts. Most tidbits involved the weather.

'Did you see that hail last night? It was coming down up at our place as big as goddam oranges with bits sticking out like a conker. I put one in the freezer.'

'Pissing down at our place.'

'…snow on the tops. We'll get another blast tonight I reckon.'

'Arthur's could be closed. Bloody treacherous.'

'There's a whole fence flattened down the coast a bit. Couldn't have been put in right in the first place.'

'Jersey breeders meetin' tomorrow…'

And then the rain came down more heavily than I had ever heard it before, beating on the tin roof like an out-of-control percussion ensemble – a tattoo of such volume that it left my ears ringing and my mind in no doubt as to my location. It could only rain like that on the coast.

Some years earlier I'd walked the Heaphy Track, north of Karamea, with my son Toby and a bunch of mates. Among them was Derek, a marvellous friend – honest, maverick, a raconteur and poet, a wild dreamer, motorbike fanatic, musician and dope smoker. It was just before Derek's illness was diagnosed. He had a wonderful time and so had we with him.

Derek died horribly, slowly, bravely of motor neurone disease.

He had always railed against rich bastards, toffs, lawyers, God botherers, poofs and private-school graduates – and yet there were more of these at his funeral than anyone else and they loved him dearly. The funeral service was taken by one of his best friends, a lawyer and a member of the Salvation Army. Derek had a way of making people examine everything about themselves but he never knew he had the gift.

I wanted to recreate something of the last day of our Heaphy tramp and so, despite the weather, I decided to walk the end section of the track, which began about 30 kilometres north of Karamea and ran for 16 kilometres along the coast to Heaphy hut. For Derek I trudged in the stinging rain through forests of nikau palms, stony streams and soggy bush, and across clingy-sand beaches and rocky headlands with water percolating down my neck.

Toby, Derek and I had left the hut last that morning. Our stomachs were empty because we'd run out of food. We had one Moro bar between us and a handful of cooked rice for breakfast. And so when we came to the first stretch of beach we tore mussels from the rocks, lit a fire, cooked them up in the billy and fell upon them like scrapping hyenas. Along the track a bit Derek cut me a stick to use as a prop over the rough bits. His commitment to the task as he whittled down the ends to blunt them was worthy of a boy scout. Derek loved the notion of self-sufficiency.

We were tired, footsore and still hungry, and to keep our spirits up we sang about food to the tune of the verse of 'Waltzing Matilda'.

Stee-ak and bananas, jam and toast and lots of chips
We'll get them all at the end of the day.
And there's peas and potatoes, sausages, all sorts of dips
We'll be as fat as a horse in the hay.

It may be more traditional when we speak of the dead to mention successes and milestones and kind deeds, but the Derek I will always have in my memory is marching resolutely along the Heaphy Track in his blue Swanndri, limping slightly from an old hip injury, his peaked cap askew, singing with gusto in a voice that is gruff and rather out of tune. Anything else is just words.

Bill displayed some laudable fortitude of his own while I was undertaking this sodden expedition. He stayed back at the Kohaihai shelter to read in the truck, but the spectacular forces of nature seduced him with his camera into the teeth of the wind. The elemental energy that caused the sea to hurl spume high in the air and cast a misty haze along the coast, that rumbled and thundered and split the sky with flashes of lightning, was not merely awesome, it was outrageous and somehow ungraspable. The photographs he took captured something of this but you had to be in it – to be ravaged by its random fury – to begin to understand its might.

We really tried to give Karamea a chance. We waited for six days for the rain to cease. God created the world in that time; we spent it in the caravan while the rain drizzled, dripped, spat or rapped on the roof. We slept and wrote and read and ate, and watched television. We also had a think-tank about what we might do next. We played 'Could we live there?' and 'Could we sell the house?' and 'How do we earn a living?' and 'What about Australia?' and 'Should we buy a bus?'

On the sixth afternoon the rain eased suddenly and Bill, who had been growing increasingly impatient and had started pacing up and down – a futile exercise in a caravan – put on his jacket and went for a walk.

'I may be some time,' he grinned as he closed the door.

Half an hour later the rain set in again and this time it was accompanied by a menacing rumble of thunder. Bill appeared at the door, dripping like a melting iceblock.

'This weather is absolutely vile,' he said. 'I can't stand this bloody place any longer.'

'Where we gonna go?'

'Anywhere away from the coast. Christchurch maybe,' he said. 'I'd like a whiff of city life for a bit. I feel like a decent cup of coffee and a damned good steak, and a movie.'

He made a lightning decision. 'In fact, I want to bugger off – right now.'

So we did.

A month later it was October and warm with spring weather. With so little between us and the elements they had a profound effect on our moods, and the change of season brought with it a lightness of spirit. Softer spring with puffy winds and myriad colours encouraged us to head south again. We decided to spend some time by the sea at Akaroa and then in the early summer to head for the hills and to lose ourselves again among the immensity of some of those wild and solitary landscapes. We would go because going was the point; and then we'd keep going – maybe forever.

For the time Bill and I had been itinerants in our own country, the wanderings in my head had been as varied as the physical journey. I'd learnt a thing or two but I'd not come to any earth-shattering conclusions. If ever I had thought that having space to think would allow me to untangle the confusions of my life, I was comprehensively wrong. But I had a lot more memories in place and perhaps in the end it's the memories themselves, rather than making sense of them, that are important. And I did learn one thing for sure – that when you start something you never know where it's going to end.